My New Business

PEARSON

At Pearson, we believe in learning – all kinds of learning for all kinds of people. Whether it's at home, in the classroom or in the workplace, learning is the key to improving our life chances.

That's why we're working with leading authors to bring you the latest thinking and best practices, so you can get better at the things that are important to you. You can learn on the page or on the move, and with content that's always crafted to help you understand quickly and apply what you've learned.

If you want to upgrade your personal skills or accelerate your career, become a more effective leader or more powerful communicator, discover new opportunities or simply find more inspiration, we can help you make progress in your work and life.

Pearson is the world's leading learning company. Our portfolio includes the Financial Times and our education business, Pearson International.

Every day our work helps learning flourish, and wherever learning flourishes, so do people.

To learn more, please visit us at **www.pearson.com/uk**

My New Business

A busy woman's guide to start-up success

WENDY KERR

Harlow, England • London • New York • Boston • San Francisco • Toronto • Sydney • Auckland • Singapore • Hong Kong
Tokyo • Seoul • Taipei • New Delhi • Cape Town • São Paulo • Mexico City • Madrid • Amsterdam • Munich • Paris • Milan

PEARSON EDUCATION LIMITED
Edinburgh Gate
Harlow CM20 2JE
United Kingdom
Tel: +44 (0)1279 623623
Web: www.pearson.com/uk

First published 2014 (print and electronic)

Pearson Education is not responsible for the content of third-party internet sites.

ISBN: 978–1–292–01622–1 (print)
         978–1–292–01624–5 (PDF)
         978–1–292–01625–2 (ePub)
         978–1–292–01623–8 (eText)

British Library Cataloguing-in-Publication Data
A catalogue record for the print edition is available from the British Library

Library of Congress Cataloging-in-Publication Data
A catalog record for the print edition is available from the Library of Congress

10 9 8 7 6 5 4 3 2 1
18 17 16 15 14

Cover design by Rob Day
Typeset in 9.5/13pt ITC Giovanni Std by 30
Print edition printed and bound in Great Britain by Henry Ling Ltd., at the Dorest Press, Dorchester, Dorset

NOTE THAT ANY PAGE CROSS REFERENCES REFER TO THE PRINT EDITION

Contents

Part 3 How do I plan for success?

Part 4 How will the business operate?

Part 5 How do I do it all?

About the author

Wendy Kerr is passionate about changing the way work works. She is on a mission to fuel 10,000 women to create a business that allows them to live the life they love.

With a 20-year career in multinational blue chip organisations, she has specialised in creating and launching new businesses around the world. Her business experience includes:

- starting a digital content business in London, expanding it to three offices globally and acquiring three media companies
- general manager of FT.com personal finance, leading the business and team of 120 through the dot-com crash, restructuring it for profitability
- starting an online share trading site in Australia and listing it on the Australian Stock Exchange, raising $70 million at the start of the first dot-com boom in the 90s.

A Corporate Crossover herself, Wendy left her corporate career to create a successful six-figure coaching and consulting business, running it from London and Tokyo. She works with leaders of high-growth, global technology companies in challenging times of expansion and change. Client companies include Expedia, IBM and Betfair.

Driven by her desire to change the way work works, she has also coached, mentored and fuelled over 1,500 women to create a business that allows them to live the life they love.

Her company, Corporate Crossovers®, enables women, wherever they are on their journey between leaving their job and starting their own business, successfully providing them with structure, tools, processes and one-on-one mentoring.

She leads a vibrant and dynamic community of Corporate Crossovers around the world who are focused on creating the life they want, providing even more support, ideas and advice for the journey.

Being true to her mission of enabling women to create businesses to support the life they love, she recently fulfilled a long-held dream of living in the south of France and travelling through Europe and the US in an RV with her family, all while running her six-figure business remotely.

A frequent media commentator, Wendy was interviewed on BBC Radio 4 Woman's Hour discussing her research on how women are changing the way work works. She was featured in *The Japan Times* discussing the role of coaching in life and career transition. Wendy also writes regularly for *The Guardian* (UK), *The Business* (Sweden) and *Women Unlimited Worldwide* on how to create a business that enables you to live the life you love.

You can connect with Wendy at:

Email: wendy@corporatecrossovers.com

Web: www.corporatecrossovers.com

Twitter: @wendy_kerr

LinkedIn: uk.linkedin.com/in/wendyrkerr/

Facebook Page: www.facebook.com/CorporateCrossovers

Author acknowledgements

This book had a team to build it and bring it to life. I would love to give thanks to my team at Pearson: Nicole, Lucy, Natasha and Paul who believed in writing a business book just for women, and pursued the idea vigorously to get a green light. They have crafted my words and ideas into a book that is practical and approachable for any woman wanting to start up her own business. And to the team at Pearson College and Mumsnet who trusted me to deliver their online entrepreneurship course and ignited the idea for this book.

To my dream team, Kim, Sam, and Lisa, all who have supported my book and business in their unique ways, and continue to believe in Corporate Crossovers, even when I falter. And to Kim who organised the interviews and logistics behind the scenes, allowing me to do what I love most: discussing women's businesses with the founders.

To my friends and family around the world, who were patient during the time I hunkered away and wrote – and for my husband taking over all the day to day tasks of the family so I could retire to the tree house that is my office and write.

Most of all I want to thank all the inspiring women I interviewed for this book. I know how busy you all are, and you gave up your time to share your business start- up experiences with me, so others could learn. Your generosity of spirit is fabulous!

And lastly, I acknowledge all the women business owners that I have met and worked with over the last decade. All of you have given me pause for thought, to learn and be inspired by your story. I want to wish you all much success in your ventures.

Introduction

Starting your own business is an incredible feat. You create something out of nothing, face your fears and go on to build an income that may support you and your family.

While the latest TV shows are encouraging us to be the next entrant on the Sunday Times Rich List or to be like Lord Sugar, many of us are motivated to start our businesses for very different reasons.

Most women business owners I have worked with over the years don't want to be Donald Trump, Lord Sugar or even Sir Richard Branson. They start their own business to be more in control of their lives, to do work that matters to them and in a way that aligns with their values. Hardly the stuff of gripping reality TV.

From research I conducted of 300 women who left their jobs to set up their businesses (I call them Corporate Crossovers), the number one reason why they did this was to escape the toxic culture. They weren't driven by the yearning to be an entrepreneur, nor did they have a killer idea, they simply wanted a different work life. They wanted more freedom and flexibility over how they spent their time and control over what they did and who they worked with.

I have had my own business for 11 years and I fell into it quite unwillingly. My husband had accepted a job in Tokyo, and at that time I was enjoying a senior management position in a FTSE 100 in London. Well, if I'm honest, enjoying it was an overstatement; surviving the politics and massive egos is closer to the truth, but I enjoyed the title and the money. In our move to

Tokyo, I became an unwilling Corporate Crossover as I couldn't get a job there, no matter how hard I tried. I retrained as a coach, and set up my company. Work flowed in; quickly my client roster became full and I had a waiting list! It was an easy start to being an entrepreneur.

Two years later we moved back to London. Upon my return I prevaricated for 18 months about whether to get a job or keep going with my executive coaching business. I wanted the money and the perceived security of a job, but in every interview I would have flashbacks to the fights and insidious behaviour of my former colleagues and decided that I couldn't bear the thought of returning to corporate life with its inherent politics and egos.

Years later, as I redefined my coaching business to focus on working with other Corporate Crossovers, I realised that I am not alone in wanting to leave that side of the corporate world. Most women who decide to set up their own business desire a life they control, even if it comes at a financial cost.

The other surprising fact from my research of 300 female Corporate Crossovers, is that 68 per cent of them were making less in their business than in their last job. Yet, two-thirds of these women would still not go back to corporate life even if they were offered more money. In that one finding, I realised that having your own business is not just about the money – it is all the other intangibles that we hold dear that matter more.

Having been a coach for 11 years, I am naturally curious and I was intrigued as to why all these successful women couldn't make the same money in their businesses as they were in their jobs. With a bit more delving, I discovered that the majority of them didn't do any planning for their business when they started, they just began.

No plan. No plan to succeed or, for that matter, no plan to fail either. With no plan and no due consideration about what life they wanted to create or the business they were birthing meant they just moved from day to day, working very hard and frustrated that they weren't making the money they used to.

My passion is to get women to do what they love and earn what they are worth. That's why I created Corporate Crossovers®, so you don't have to be in the 68 per cent. From my experience of starting companies both for myself and corporate (I was general manager of a dot-com start-up in Sydney and raised $70 million for it on the Australian Stock Exchange, and my executive coaching business has earnt consistently over six figures), I know how important it is to have a plan before you press 'send' on your resignation email, or enrol the children into expensive daycare, to start the business of your dreams.

This book is all about the plan. The plan for your business and also for your life that will surround the business. Chances are, you have other responsibilities. Maybe you are the key carer for older parents, or children. Or maybe you have a passion that needs more time than just weekends and holidays for you to pursue it fully. When you are starting to think about creating a business, you need to think about how you will run it in conjunction with what you want to do with your life.

This is your chance to create a life the way you want it – how many days you work, what hours, who you work with and how you manage the personal side of your life. A plan for your business will allow you to consider all of this, as well as be confident the business will succeed.

When we wrap the business plan inside the life we want to create, then we feel more compelled to make it happen. The rewards won't just be financial but be heart felt as well.

This book is designed to walk you step by step through the planning process, so you will have the clarity, and confidence to commit to starting the business and your new life. It's full of templates, real-life stories from women who have been there before you, and simple explanations of that stuff you know you need to know, but, it all seems a bit dull.

To help you bring this book to life I have posted various tools and templates on my website: **www.CorporateCrossovers.com/ MyNewBusiness.**

You will see this Worksheet icon whenever the Worksheet is available online and can be downloaded and printed at the above website.

 Other exercises are more reflective, and require you to take notes; these will be identified by a Notes icon.

Together, the Notes and Worksheets will provide you with a fantastic plan to start your business. Create a folder, real or virtual, to collect and collate all your notes and scribblings. It will be an invaluable resource for you to refer back to as you go on your journey to start up.

Download the Worksheets and templates as you read through the book. They will guide you through the steps of starting up your business simply and effectively.

Other free resources available on the website are my blog, video tips and podcasts, all designed to help you feel confident and prepared to start your business.

I want you to use this book as a guide, a reference that you keep coming back to. Business evolves and changes, and so your business plan must too. The best business plans are dynamic and evolving, with a strong framework and a steady goal.

This book is meant to be a living, breathing guide as you start your new business. As you go through the book, your knowledge of starting a business will deepen and so your thoughts and ideas on what you want to create may change as you go along. And that's fine. Remember, there are no right or wrong answers; it will be an evolving process.

It would delight me if you scribble notes all over the book, buy a beautiful notebook to capture your thoughts, or have a file on your computer or device to capture your thinking and inspirations.

My mission is to enable 10,000 women to create a business that allows them to live the life they love. I hope this book ignites your journey!

Part 1

Is starting a business right for me?

Before we delve into the business ideas, profit and loss statements and market research, let's take a step back and consider what you really want your life to be like, and why you want to have a business. Knowing this will give you a firm foundation upon which to create your new business.

From all of my work with business owners and research for my books, I know that the most successful are those who are crystal clear on what role their business plays in their life, and their motivations for starting it.

Chapter

Do I really want this?

This chapter is all about introspection and discovery. From working through this chapter you will discover:

- how to design a new life
- what your values are and how to reconnect with them
- the real reason why you want to start a business.

Chances are, if you are reading this book, you want change in your life. It may be that you have a job that no longer satisfies you as it did before, and you are yearning to do something more meaningful. Or maybe you love what you do, but the environment in which you work is toxic and you want to work in a way aligned with your values. Perhaps you have decided that being a full-time mum is no longer for you, as you crave more challenge and your own income.

These may or may not represent your situation, but it is the desire for a different life that drives our quest to start a new business.

You know you want a change, and sense that getting a new job isn't really the answer. So you ponder starting your own business.

Getting clear on the life you want to create is an essential foundation step in starting your new business. Without this, you may end up creating a new life by default that replicates the life you wanted to reject. And what's the point of that? Long hours, little pay and no clear boundaries between your work and personal time. Frankly, that doesn't sound like a scenario worth throwing in your job for. Too often I have seen women start businesses and they end up working harder and for less money than when they had a job.

It doesn't have to be this way.

Now is a fabulous opportunity to take some time and think about your life. The sad fact is that most of us spend more time planning our summer vacations than we do our lives. So it's your chance now to grab this moment to take control and think about the life you really want, instead of the life you may be currently tolerating.

Tiffany London, founder of Tiffany Rose, creators of special occasion maternity wear, describes how she knew it was time to change her life: '*I had been working for many years in the corporate world which spanned across many different fields. It was creative, it was finance, it was graphic design, interior design, it was PR and event management. After doing that for a number of years I decided that I just wanted to do something different and I didn't know what. I just knew that I didn't want to do this anymore. I realised that I had to do something of my own where I could actually control it and be really passionate about it.*

My elder sister was pregnant and she had her best friend's wedding to go to and she really struggled to find something wonderful to wear. I tried helping her find things online and I was struggling too. I think it was a combination of lots of different things that made me think, "You know, I could do this," and I think I was just at that stage in my life when I thought, "Do you know what? I'm going to give it a go."'

I find that when I ask women clients the question, 'If you could have anything you wanted, what would it be?' that they often struggle to answer. Years of putting others first – children, partners, parents, or their jobs – means that there is little time to even think of the question, let alone formulate an answer. What they want is deeply buried below everyone else's needs and wants. Yet what they feel is a growing dissatisfaction and the sense that something needs to change.

Often this dissatisfaction is because parts of their lives are not aligned with their values. Our values are our deeply held beliefs or ideals about how our lives should be lived. When we have a value conflict, or our values aren't being met, we can feel uneasy, frustrated or even angry. Sometimes it is evident when our values are not being met, other times we just feel a dis-ease.

It is this feeling of dissatisfaction, a sense that something could be different, that leads many women to start their own business, whether they dislike their job, or know that they could be doing more on top of looking after the children.

Sandra Roycroft-Davis, Harley St behavioural expert and founder of Thinking Slimmer describes how her deep values clash led her to discover her new business: *'It was purely by accident because I was in PR and celebrity management. When I was running my PR company I had charity clients, and then I moved into celebrity management. While it was all very exciting, if I'm honest the values weren't working for me. I got very disillusioned with that industry. I had a big values clash as celebrity management was all about money and I don't get out of bed every day just to make money.* 'During her period of questioning what she could do next, Sandra went on an NLP course: *'I discovered NLP. When I was on the NLP course I decided I wanted to take that further and train to be a cognitive hypnotherapist.'* Sandra started practising cognitive hypnotherapy but she wanted to do more: *'I found it wasn't enough for me just dealing with one-on-ones when I had so much wealth of knowledge in how to do public relations, so I then thought, "Right, what am I going to do?"'*

She had observed that many of her clients were coming to see her for weight loss, and came to the conclusion that she could package the approach she was using and help more people in their desire to lose weight. She says: '*Because obesity is such a problem and I know that I can make a difference, I created Slim Pod.*'

Thinking Slimmer is now the official national partner of Change4Life, the Department of Health's lifestyle and wellbeing campaign, and is the first company in the world to commission independent clinical trials into the effectiveness of voice recordings using unconscious persuasion to help people lose weight.

What are my values?

When we are creating our own business, it is a great opportunity to ensure that our work lives are aligned with our values. We are creating something new, so we owe it to ourselves to honour our values.

At this early stage of starting your new business, take the time to assess and reflect on your inner self. It's time to be introspective and create strong inner foundations for your business. Answers to questions about your values and the life you want will be fundamental to making this leap into entrepreneurship a success.

You will probably have an intuitive sense of what your values are. Use the following Worksheet to bring them to the surface and make them tangible. These will provide a strong bellwether for future decisions.

Clarifying your personal values

Step 1: Develop a shortlist of your top values

Review the list of words below. Circle 20 words which resonate with you as being important to live your life by. If there is a word missed that represents you more fully, then add it in.

Abundance	Flexibility	Optimism	Safety
Activism	Forgiveness	Order	Security
Advancement	Style	Passion	Self-control
Adventure	Friendship	Patriotism	Self-respect
Aesthetics	Fun	Persistence	Sensuality
Ambition	Generosity	Tolerance	Spirituality
Art	Trust	Empathy	Spontaneity
Stability	Growth	Wealth	Physical challenge
Authenticity	Happiness	Play	Influencing people
Balance	Harmony	Pleasure	Time freedom
Beauty	Having a voice	Power	Financial security
Calmness	Having dreams	Process	Experimentation
Challenge	Health	Nature	Quality of life
Change	Help others	Love	Trustworthiness
Charity	Help society	Tranquility	Protecting environment
Collaboration	Honesty	Quality	Living your dreams
Comfort	Honour	Recognition	Attention to detail
Community	Humour	Directness	Relationship with partner
Compassion	Imagination	Reliability	Making a difference
Competence	Independence	Respect	Global awareness
Competition	Learning	Results	Open communication
Courage	Inner harmony	Risk taking	Determination
Creativity	Innovation	Risk adverse	Personal expression
Laughter	Inspiring others	Equality	Cultural diversity
Curiosity	Integrity	Excitement	Personal growth
Decisiveness	Intelligence	Fairness	Professionalism
Democracy	Kindness	Expertise	Leadership
Fashion	Knowledge	Family	Freedom of choice

Now make a list of what your twenty main values are.

Step 2: Discover your five key values

Uncover your five key values by reviewing the twenty listed above as follows:

1. Circle together values that are similar.
2. Delete those that seem irrelevant now.
3. Prioritise your top five and list them in order of importance.

Helen Pattinson, co-founder and director of Montezuma's Chocolates, along with her husband, decided that they wanted a very different life. Previously lawyers in busy London law firms, they set off travelling. *'When we left our lives as lawyers in London we promised each other that we wouldn't go back to doing that once we got home from South America. We decided that we would love to have our own business but we didn't have a clue what that would be in. So while we were travelling we were looking for ideas and chocolate just kept hitting home. We didn't really have any concept of what that would look like while we were travelling but as soon as we returned we started researching the chocolate industry.'*

Fourteen years later, Montezuma's is established as Britain's leading and most innovative family luxury chocolate maker, selling in its own stores across the country and in leading retailers.

What do you want?

Now you are reacquainted with your deeply held beliefs about your life and your view of the world, what do you want? If you could design your life any way you wanted – what would it be like?

This isn't about throwing the baby out with the bathwater, as I know there will be some parts of your life that you love. So how do you have more of this, and how can starting your own business facilitate this?

Thinking about this at such an early stage of your business development means that you will remain more cognisant of what the business needs to deliver to you in terms of lifestyle. You can actively design it this way to achieve that.

Before you get overwhelmed with the vastness of the question, I've made it easy for you. Take some time out and consider the questions on the following Worksheet.

Your ideal life

For some this will be easy, for others it will be nail-bitingly difficult – if the latter is the case you may want to revisit it a few times.

1. **What do you love about your life as it is now?** It could be things like your health, your partner, where you live, your weekly yoga class. You get the picture … jot down the ten things you love about your life right now.

2. **What frustrates you about your life, and what don't you enjoy?** It could be your boss, the length of your working day, not spending enough time with your children, commuting, not enough travel. List 10 items now.

3. **What can you change?** From the 10 items you listed in Step 2 above, what can you change? An example might be the weather in London, but you love living in that city, so you decide to put up with it. Something you may want to change is commuting to work. What are those items that you can actually do something about, as opposed to accepting them? Circle them.

4. **What's missing in your life?** This is time to dig deep into what you want. Reach down and pull out your pushed-aside wants and bring them to the surface. What do you want that you currently don't have? Write down 10 things. It may be elements such as time to be more creative, to rediscover a musical passion, to exercise, to do more meaningful work, or just to have fun!

5. **Bringing it together.** By now you will have a clearer idea of what you love, dislike and want in your life. It's now time to craft an outline of what you want in your ideal life. An easy way to do this is to look at the three lists and write down all those elements you desire in your life.

6. As you write these down, chances are other thoughts and ideas will come into your mind. That's great – add these in too!

7. Jot everything down in your notebook.

8. **What will it feel like?** Now you have created a picture of how your life could be, write down how it makes you feel. Imagine this is how your life is, and consider what it feels like to be living this life every day. What are your emotions, what are you loving about it, how does your work play a part in this life?

Spending time sketching out your ideal life will give you a benchmark to check new ideas against. You will need to consider if they align with what you want from your life. For instance if you want to spend more time at home and reduce travelling time, then you would want a business that could be home-based, not one that involves visiting clients abroad.

Alicia Cowan, online marketing guru at www.aliciacowan.com, has created a thriving enterprise helping business owners all over the world use internet marketing strategies and tools to grow their income. She runs her business from her homes in London and Ibiza.

Alicia was very clear about her vision for her business from the start. She says: '*I always knew that I had a vision to create a location-independent business, serving other people. I didn't want to manage staff, I wanted to keep it small and keep the costs low. I wanted the business to enable me to have the life that I wanted and that's what I have created.*'

Why do I want a business?

Not only do you need to consider what you want your life to be as a result of this business but also why you want to have your own business. Starting up a new business is exhilarating, stimulating and fun. But it can also be draining in terms of time, energy and money. It may even impact your relationships, your health and other opportunities.

Before you fully commit to starting a business, or if you have already made the leap, it is imperative that you get clear on your big reason why you have created this business.

Knowing why will:

- give you the fuel to keep on going with the business when you go through slumps and unexpected twists and turns
- keep you going in your darkest hour, when you think of throwing it all in
- be deeply held, and align with your key values
- help you make sense of your life, and allow you to live the life you want.

You can then build your business on your terms, and be aligned with what is truly important to you.

You may have a burning desire to be financially free, and want to create a large enterprise, or maybe you want to start a business that gives you freedom and flexibility to use your time how you want. Perhaps you want to leave a legacy, something for future generations to experience, or you have a yearning to share your creativity with the world. It may be that you want to create a business that is ethical and contributes back to the community.

Your reason why will be individual to you.

Hayley Gait-Golding, founder of BEAR, a £18 million food business, is very clear on her reason why. Working as a personal trainer, she worked with her clients not only on their fitness but also on eating healthier. She says: *'My clients were so confused about their food choices, it was just so boring for them. I was really uninspired by everything in the supermarkets. I started looking at ingredients in a little more detail and saw how much nonsense is in there. If you turned over the back of a cereal packet, how many ingredients are in there and how many you couldn't pronounce.'*

She goes on to say: *'We are eating all these awful processed foods with all these awful unspeakable ingredients that we don't understand, so I felt really, really passionate about changing that. I wanted to change modern processed foods into things that were nature's alternatives and that's where the idea of BEAR came from.'*

Your reasons for starting a business

To help you gain clarity on your reasons for starting a business, ask yourself these questions:

1. Why is the business or idea important?
2. What difference will it make to you?
3. What difference will it make to your customers?
4. What do you want to be saying about your business in 12 months?
5. How does it align with your key values?
6. Why do you want to start this business?

After completing the three Worksheets in this chapter, you will be clearer on what you want your life to be like as a result of starting this business and how you will feel about it. Having this knowledge will give you the confidence to step forward and make it happen!

Justine Roberts, founder of Mumsnet, the biggest network for parents in the UK, founded in 2000, talks about her reason for starting Mumsnet, which continues to be evident in the network today: '*I have always believed in the wisdom of real people versus the gurus. Particularly around this area of parenting as it often seemed to me that mothers and women were being told what to do by men with qualifications after their name, and not really trusting their instincts. Mumsnet gives a voice to real people who have been there and done that, and treats them as just as important a voice as the experts.*'

Busy woman's shortcut

To help you get moving quickly, I've included a shortcut at the end of each chapter However, I'm afraid there's no 'Busy woman's shortcut'for this chapter, because this phase of reflection is critical and not something we often do. Take some time to be introspective and enjoy the process!

Caution

Don't skip the steps in this chapter even if you are in a hurry to get going with your idea. Running a business is like being on a never ending personal development programme. The more you understand about yourself and what you really want the stronger the foundation you have for moving forward.

Be savvy

If you don't already, start acquiring some practices to support you. During a time of change you need to have deep internal reserves to call on. I recommend doing things like:

- drinking lots of water
- finding time to meditate (and if you hate the thought of it, find some five-minute guided meditations on iTunes – they are a great way to get started)
- exercising
- writing a journal – this is a great way to clear your head by writing down your thoughts daily.

These techniques are all designed to help you move forward, gain perspective and stay grounded.

Chapter

Do I have a good idea?

At its simplest, business is about creating something that someone will buy for more than it cost you to make. Having a compelling and relevant idea is the foundation for a successful business.

In this chapter you will discover:

- the four ways to find a business idea if you don't already have one
- how to crystallise your idea if it's a bit fuzzy
- why feedback is essential, even at this early stage.

Is finding that killer business idea an art or a science?

You have determined that running your business is what you want to do to give you the life you desire and be aligned with your innermost beliefs.

But what will you actually do? What will you create that someone will pay for?

Since you are reading this book, you may have a vague idea of what you want to do. Maybe you have your idea tightly defined and are already imagining who will buy from you. Or you could be at the other end of the spectrum, knowing that you want to create a business but not having quite found that killer idea.

How do people come up with business ideas they love and that are successful? Why is it that some ideas you hear of, you know are destined for success, and others are quickly assigned to the wastebasket?

From my in-depth interviews of over 50 successful Corporate Crossovers for my first book, and my coaching work with many business owners over the years, I have discovered there are four ways that business owners discover that magic idea. And they are all a combination of art, science, luck and great timing.

Four ways to discover your new business idea[1]

1 Epiphany

Epiphanies are a bit like buses – there is never one around when you need one, and then three turn up all at once. The 'light bulb moment' will happen when you least expect it, typically in the shower, as your brain churns through lots of disparate pieces of information, making sense of it all. Then 'kapow', you have that light bulb moment, and suddenly you get that idea or insight about what to do next.

Blippar is a new app that enables users to scan products and unleash special interactive content on their device. It is coveted by advertisers and ad agencies to make their products and campaigns more compelling.

Jessica Butcher, co-founder and CMO of Blippar, describes how she had an amazing idea to commercialise the technology her co-founders

---

1 Take from research findings of my first book *Corporate Crossovers: When it's time to leave the office*, Momentum Coaching Change Management Ltd, 2014

created: *'They were just playing around with technology and ideas and the hallelujah moment came when they managed to change the Queen's head on a five pound note into my co-founder Rish's head. We came back with a brilliant business idea to take that technology to those who mattered, the advertisers, media owners, and start converting the physical advertising and print media into very fun experiences. And from there it's all snowballed really.'*

2 Leverage your experience

Doing more of what you love and what you are good at is also a solid way to build a new business. You may have been an HR director for the past ten years, and love developing people and leading change. You also have a great list of contacts in the industry. It would be easy for you to leverage your expertise and network to create an HR consulting business.

Keren Lerner, founder of Top Left Design, a leading web design consultancy which has created over 600 websites, shares how she went from an employee to owning her own company: *'I was working as a designer at a web design company for three years and I really liked my job. But they grew too fast in the wake of the dot-com bubble bursting and eventually everyone got made redundant and the company closed. I had three options: to find a new job, go freelance or contract – I tried all three.*

Jobs in the industry were scarce at the time, and I did try contracting but it seemed a waste of my skills – much of the time was spent waiting for feedback. When working on my own freelance projects, I finish the next step of a project, send it back to the client, work on another part of another project – always keeping the ball in the client's court.' As Keren started to network more, she got more projects, and then her agency Top Left Design was born.

3 Solve a problem

Fed up with a product or service in the market? Think you could do it better? Maybe you could. Or perhaps you keep wishing that someone had invented something that would make your life easier. Take some time to think about what you wish for, or what frustrates you, and that could be the beginning of your new idea.

Dr Kate Hersov, co-founder and deputy CEO of Medikidz, the world's first medical education initiative for young people, describes how her business ideas sparked. *'The idea came from frustration that my colleague and I felt as clinicians dealing with young people. We never had anything to provide them to help them understand what was happening and to take away some of the fear they may be feeling.'*

That frustration has grown into Medikidz, which now distributes more than three million publications into 50 countries, in 28 different languages. Each of the Medikidz publications feature the 'Medikidz' – a gang of five superheroes, each of whom specialise in different areas of the human body and demystify common children's illnesses.

4 Follow your passion

What do you love? What do your friends always ask for your opinion on? What are you always reading and learning about? What do you lose yourself in? If you are passionate about something, you will know a lot more about it than anyone else. How can you turn this knowledge into a compelling business idea?

Critical to this stage of developing a business is to keep an open mind, keep observing and maintain a sense of wonder. Always be asking yourself 'what if?

Cleopatra Browne, founder and chief guide of Celtic Quest Coasteering, lives and breathes coasteering (climbing, scrambling, swimming and jumping along a coast). She started her business after working for a local outdoor company. She tells her story: *'The outdoor industry is a lifestyle choice in that I love playing in the sea. I saw the opportunity to take this activity and do it better than everyone else. The money was obviously important and my initial maths said that I would earn more doing it this way than working for someone else so that was a bonus. So was being my own boss.'*

Now you have some proven ways of discovering an idea for your business, use these questions below as a prompt to fuel your imagination.

Finding your idea

1. **What epiphanies have you had**? Think about what ideas and inspirations you have had, for example when taking a shower or when on a walk. These may be related to ideas you have had for new products or where you have seen a gap in the market that no one else has filled. Note down any flashes of inspirations you have had.

2. **Leveraging your experience.** What previous jobs have you had that you loved? What skills and talents do you most enjoy using?

3. **Solving a problem.** What frustrates you? What do you know could be done better? What problems do your friends or family have that could be solved? Write down your ideas.

4. **Passions.** What do you love? What passions have been dormant since school? What do friends always ask your advice on? Write down everything you feel passionate about.

Turning a vague notion into a valid idea

Many ideas and opportunities will flood your brain as you start to consider your new business venture. As you imagine who your customer will be, ideas will keep tumbling into your brain, along with great ways to make more money, augment your business and be a success. But then you look at your notes and realise that you have created a monster and lost sight of the original idea.

This is a very common scenario when we first start planning our new business. We don't want to limit the business potential and scope as we have a compulsion to maximise our business idea.

The trap with this is that we can create a business concept that is unfocused, unclear and confusing. We develop a proposition that is hard to articulate in a single sentence. Sales are slow to eventuate, as a confused prospect never buys.

How do you harness these opposing forces? On the one hand your unbridled enthusiasm and energy generates new ideas and fuels your effort. But on the other hand, your concept becomes overwhelming and difficult to find a way into.

Try this three-step approach to keep your energy levels high in order to capture your flashes of inspiration and then to distil them into a tight business concept.

Step 1: Create an ideas bank

This could be a notebook, a file on your device, or a notebook on Evernote. Use this space to deposit:

- all of your ideas
- brainwaves
- inspirations
- observations.

Write freely, don't censor! An idea that may seem irrelevant now may be extremely useful in 12 months' time.

As you are in your business-creation stage, take time every day to ponder what's in your ideas bank. Think about:

- what else could be added
- where an idea could lead to
- what else is happening in this space.

Remember, all ideas are great ideas at this stage, so no matter how outrageous an idea seems, write it down.

You never know, tomorrow the idea that you were going to delete, may be the idea that leads to another idea that then becomes that killer concept you have been searching for.

Get into the habit of setting time aside for you to think, dream and consider. The most common complaint from business owners is that they never get enough time to work 'on' the business. Start now, and make it a good habit that you keep as you embark on this journey.

Ideas bank

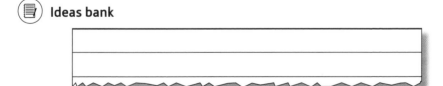

Step 2: What does your customer want to buy?

When we have a business, the idea is one half of the equation for success. The other half, and equally important, is ensuring that someone will buy what we are selling. I know this sounds obvious, but too often I have worked with disappointed and frustrated business owners who are passionate about their idea and can't fathom why no one is buying it. You may know some people in this category.

Time for a mind game… Imagine you are your customer. What problems do you have that need to be solved?

Typically people pay for solutions to their problems (real or perceived). We don't buy a spade to have a spade; we actually buy the spade to dig a hole. Thus the problem we are solving here is the lack of a hole. When you buy a newspaper, you aren't buying newsprint and ink, rather you are quenching your desire for news and information.

Thinking about the problem that your ideal customer wants to solve allows you to consider your offering from their eyes. You may have even experienced the problem yourself.

Take some time to think about your idea, and what problem it is solving for your customer. What is the solution you are providing? How are you making their lives better, easier, more successful?

By considering your ideas as potential solutions, you begin to refine your thinking. Your vague notion sharpens up and begins to take shape.

 What problem is your idea solving?

Think about the problems your idea may be solving and make a list.

Step 3: Adding in your sparkle!

Now you have considered your customer and their needs it's time to add in your own energy and passion!

Open up your 'ideas bank' and select those ideas that will make your offering even better for your customer. Keep thinking about the problem you are solving for them, or what solution they are buying from you. Adding in your personality and style will allow the concept to evolve and be unique.

Add in your personality and style

What makes you you? Do you love bright colours, or do you have a practical, no-nonsense approach to things? Maybe you adore illustrations or all things vintage? How can your idea truly be an expression of you? And thereby unique? Jot down all your ideas.

In Chapter 7 we will go much deeper into your target market and its specific problems but these initial foundation steps are a great start.

Keep creating new ideas!

Ideas are the lifeblood of any business. How we innovate, delight customers and beat our competition are all fuelled by great ideas. You will keep getting inspiration, so ensure your ideas file is always handy to add them in. Take some time each month to review your 'ideas bank' and see what ideas can be brought to life.

Get feedback

When you are starting to shape your business idea, it's really important to get feedback. If you don't seek others' opinions on your idea, you risk creating a beautiful offering that you adore but one that no one wants to buy.

Taking time to ask others what they think of your concept at this early stage will allow you to incorporate their feedback into the refinement of your idea. It is important to go into these feedback conversations with an open mind and to be grateful of what you are told.

Not only will you receive some opinions about your idea but you may also get some market information, contacts, new ideas and good advice.

As you develop your business offering, there will be several research stages to go through which you will discover in Part 2. As your idea takes shape, more in-depth research can be conducted, but right at the beginning, start here.

Initially begin by asking your family and friends what they think. Use the Worksheet below as a guide for your initial research. Ask them to be honest and constructive. Their answers will broaden your perspective and help you step back from your own thinking.

 ## Initial research questions

- Would you buy this product/service?
- What problem is it trying to solve?
- What do you like about it?
- What would you change about it?
- Have you seen anything like it before?
- What would you pay for it?

The more you start to talk about your idea now and get some feedback, the better your idea will become. When your idea is centred in reality and receives honest feedback, that nagging question about how good your idea is will start to dissipate.

At the initial stages of your business creation, this is a simple way to get an outside perspective on your idea, and to give you the confidence to keep moving forward.

> Jane Michell, founder of Jane Plan, a weight loss programme that provides prepared meals, started testing her business idea out for friends in her kitchen: 'All my friends used to say to me, "How come you're so skinny?" and I would say, "Well, I watch what I eat". Then I started to go to the supermarket and to do a weekly shop for a friend, pop it round to her house in my car and say, "Eat this and nothing else. I will call you on day one and I'll call you on day seven and we'll keep doing it." She lost weight, and then one friend told another and so forth and it just grew from there.' So far Jane Plan has helped over 8,000 people lose weight successfully.

Once you have got enough initial feedback, you need to compile the responses, review and reflect.

You may like to use this Worksheet to compile their responses.

 Initial research response

1. How many responses were positive?
2. What did they like?
3. What did they think needed changing?
4. Were you able to describe the idea easily?
5. Had they seen anything like it before?
6. What problem did they think you were trying to solve?
7. What prices did they mention when you asked them what they would pay for it?

Spending time at this part of the idea development cycle will save you a lot of money and time later on. And enjoy it – you will discover so much about your idea, your market and how people tick. This is the most fascinating part of starting a new business.

Caution

Naysayers... when my clients go through this stage, they will find one or two people, and often they are close friends, completely negate the idea. When this happens, it can feel treacherous. You feel as if no one supports you, and that you couldn't start a business even if you tried harder. Your confidence takes a knock.

From my experience (my own, and that of my clients) often this negative response is because you are pressing some of their buttons. They may feel envious that you are actually doing something you have dreamt of, and they really would love to do this themselves, but are too scared. Or they like you just the way you are, and may feel slightly threatened that your life will change and thus will impact on your relationship with them. These reactions will occur at a very deep and subconscious level ... but this is what may drive their negativity. If this is occurring, keep probing. Ask for clarification on why they think it won't work – remember this is all great feedback to make your idea and offering even stronger.

Busy woman's shortcut

Don't wait until a certain day to do all your research. Save time by recording ideas at every opportunity. Every time you see something that could add to your idea ... grab it! Take a photo of it, clip it, record a voice memo. Create an 'ideas bank' now.

Be savvy

Often I will have a free consultation with a prospective client who wants to start a business but they don't think they have an idea. A few minutes into our conversation and out they come! They have plenty of ideas but because they haven't been teased out before or given any energy, they can remain locked inside. Take the time to start writing your ideas down and breathe life into them.

Chapter

Do I have what it takes?

Is creating and running a business for you? In my experience I have never seen a 'get rich quick' scheme work, and typically success involves hard work and perseverance. In this chapter you will discover:

- the seven essential qualities to be a successful entrepreneur
- how you compare
- ideas to facilitate change where you need it.

Having a great idea for a business that people will pay for, of course, is essential to your business success. Equally important to that is your ability to run a business. It is not enough to be able to create gorgeous flower arrangements to be a successful florist, you also need to run a business to support that talent.

There are two components to running a business:

1. the external skills (sales, marketing, finance, operations etc.)
2. the internal attributes.

Running a business well requires the fundamental elements you would expect in business management, such as marketing, selling, managing the finances and other tasks. We will get to all of these in detail in Parts 3 and 4 of the book.

Internal traits are more important as these will make the biggest difference to the success of your business. These will determine how you persevere to get a meeting with a buyer from a large retailer, how you recover from setbacks and how you inspire and lead your staff.

From my work with hundreds of business owners and the research I have completed, I know that to run a business successfully, you need to have a mix of qualities that will enable you to nurture and drive your business through the journey, unwavering passion and determination.

Popular media would have us believe that the legendary entrepreneurs are born that way, concocting profitable deals with their schoolmates from a young age, and that you either have those elusive qualities or you don't. I don't agree. From what I have experienced over the years, you can acquire the qualities of those successful business owners, if you want to.

Seven essential qualities for business success

Last year I wrote my book *Corporate Crossovers: When it's Time to Leave the Office* (Momentum Coaching Change Management Ltd, 2014) about the journey from leaving your job to setting up your own business. I spoke to 50 successful Corporate Crossovers, and I distilled from those interviews and my work with business owners over the years, the seven essential qualities of success, which are summarised here.

1 Passion

This is the fire in your belly, total and utter belief that what you are doing will be a success. You are passionate about your idea, and the impact it will have on those that use it.

Passion will fuel you. As you travel through the peaks and troughs of the journey to create your business, the passion for your idea will pull you through the troughs and keep you motivated.

There can be times when you are running your business when you will wonder if it's all worth it and question the impact you are making. How do I know? I know because I have been in that place many times over the years, as have my clients.

These dips in belief and drive are normal and my advice for getting it back is to reflect on the difference you are making to your end user. How does what you do or create make their lives better, more enjoyable, more successful? And when you think of that impact, how do you feel?

I know that when I enable someone to take their idea from a vague notion into a fully-fledged business, I feel fulfilled, humbled and energised. I know my work matters. It's thinking about this which refuels my passion and keeps me going.

Tiffany London speaks about her passion: '*I would say you have to absolutely love it inside out. You have to be so passionate about your idea because there will be times when you hate doing what you do and so you need that passion to carry you through that to better times.*'

2 Determination

Tenacity and resilience are qualities related to determination. Not giving up at the first hurdle but instead persevering with the 'no's' until you get a 'yes'. Determination is fuelled by your passion and deep desire to make this business a reality.

Think about a time or situation when you wanted something very badly. That for whatever reason, it was critical that it happened and you got the outcome you desired. That level of determination is what you need in your new business.

Growing your determination is much easier when you know what the outcomes of your work will be, and how you will benefit from it.

Tracy Mort MBE, founder and MD of Grace Cole, creator of beautiful beauty and body care products, recalls her determination starting the business as the recession hit in 2008: *'I was so determined to succeed and we were told categorically by every man and his dog that we wouldn't. Well that was like a red rag to a bull. I knew our products would work and if we gave good service, so getting all those pieces right, surely we had to succeed. I just focused on nothing else, we had to succeed.'*

3 Optimism

This means feeling confident that your business will work, that you will find a way through difficult issues, always asking, 'What if?' and 'Could we do this?' Optimism is key in setting up a business. You need to go into business expecting the best and even when the reality is different, find creative ways to overcome it and build on it.

It's worth remembering that whilst you can't control what happens to you, you can control how you react to it. Optimism will enable you to turn adversity into an opportunity and learn from it.

A simple way to grow optimism is to take time each day and write down three things that went well. This will cause you to reflect back on the day searching for positive things to write down. Over time, you will begin to notice that you are more mindful of the good things in your day, as you will have trained your brain to look for positive happenings.

Helen from Monetzuma's shares the greatest lesson she has learnt from running the business for 14 years: *'Being positive and staying positive, sounds a bit wishy washy but it has the most enormous power. I think that we have got through bad situations just by looking on the bright side. I think it's really hard; you go through phases in the business where you get really bogged down with the nitty gritty and you can't look at the big picture. I think it is important to keep positive and keep looking onwards and upwards. I don't think our business would still be here if we weren't positive people.'*

4 Customer love

Keeping your customers coming back for more is the easiest way to build your business. Putting them at the forefront of what you do is key to this. Thinking in your decisions, 'What would the customers want?' will ensure that you are building customer love.

Valuing your customers by giving great service and consistently exceeding expectations enhances your business, and you will build customer loyalty and reduce the likelihood of them switching from you to a competitor.

To build your awareness of customer love, start to take note of what delights you when you are buying products and services. Was it the way the store staff greeted you with a genuine smile and offered to help, or maybe it was the perfume sprayed on the tissue as you bought your favourite beauty product from the big department store?

Whatever it may be, start to collect these examples and think about how they make you feel. Then you will know what it's like to be on the receiving end of customer love, and this will make it easier for you to implement.

As Jane from Jane Plan advises: '*You have to always exceed your customers' expectations and that's the way they will tell their friends. If you do something that surprises them, obviously, it makes them think, 'This is so much better that I could have even possibly hoped for". They'll only tell their friends if there's a real "Wow, this is amazing!"*

5 Courage

Opportunities are everywhere but you have to be fearless to grab them! Starting and running your own business will push and pull at every part of your comfort zone. You will have to put yourself out there in ways you haven't imagined. There is no company brand to lean on anymore, no sales department to bring in the business. It is now completely up to you.

You need to be prepared to feel the fear when you start a business and get through it. If you are scared of something it just means that you're being stretched out of what you have done before. Take a breath, consider if this is the best course of action for your business, and if so, then push your fear to one side and proceed.

If you are feeling timid and doubt is setting in about how fearless you could really be, then I recommend you take a walk down memory lane. Somewhere in your past will be an experience where you demonstrated how courageous you can be. It may have been recent, or maybe it was from your school days. I want you to recapture that memory and linger on the details. Ask yourself these questions to get deeply into the moment again.

- What was the situation?
- What was the time of day?
- Who else was involved?
- How did you conquer your fear and do what needed to be done?
- How did you feel once you had done it?

I recommend writing down the answers to these questions and then give this experience a name. Maybe you call it 'My fearless moment', or 'The time I pushed past my fear' – or something that is more personal to you.

Then when you need to conquer your fears as you begin your business, recapture this memory and how you felt. Remember that you have already shown this essential capability, and you can do it again.

Luisa Gonzalez, founder of Waggin' Tails Pet Boutique, Spa and Veterinary services in Chelsea knows about real and imagined fear. Held up at gunpoint in her native Venezuela, she decided to immigrate to London to start a new life. She says: *'Don't let your fears hold you back. They are just the best things that can ever happen. Be convinced and believe in the power you have to do things and change things.'*

Kay White, savvy and influential communication expert for Women in Business and founder of Way Forward Solutions has a great tip on addressing fear: 'You don't have to say yes to everything, you just say yes to the first conversation.'

From her years of experience of working with women, she believes that we can talk ourselves out of even talking about the first step with someone. She goes on to say: 'Women will, as a gender, often think "Oh my god, I can't possibly be on stage". Well, she didn't ask you to be on stage, she asked you to have a coffee about a conversation that might be about doing something next year! The key is to take the first step and then see where that leads to.'

6 Flexibility

Staying close to your customers also means that you are that much more informed about their needs and how the market may be shifting. In many cases the business you start may be different to one that you are running a few years later. The need to be nimble, to be observant, is an essential quality.

How often do you read the news, make an effort to keep up to date with the market you are interested in or seek out industry leaders' opinions? The more you do this, the more aware you will be of what the trends are. You will also have an appreciation for what's normal in your space, and so when changes do happen, you will be quick to notice.

Sandra of Thinking Slim realised that she had to flex her business model to make the impact she wanted to in the world, to reach more people and reduce obesity nationally: 'Weight loss is such a crowded market, I needed to see how I could stand out. The answer lay in gaining credibility through medical approval and gaining the attention of the NHS and health insurance companies.' Sandra's SlimPod is now halfway through medical trials and the results are looking very promising.

7 Hard work

When you are setting up your business you are creating something out of nothing. You are establishing a brand in a competitive market place, creating a presence, building a sales pipeline, getting prospects to know, like and trust you and your offering.

Starting up your own business can feel like you are working harder than ever before. You may be working longer hours than you have for some time, and earning far less money as you start to become established. Yet, all the business owners I have spoken to accept this trade-off to be their own boss, and to bring their idea to the world.

Hayley of BEAR nibbles shares about her time spent in building the business: '*I can honestly say that since I have started the business I have had maybe a couple of Sundays off, if that, and holidays that I have been on, I have worked all the way through. There isn't much spare time at all so it literally takes over your life but in a really positive way.*'

Could you do it?

Reading through this list of seven essential qualities, what were you thinking? Did you recognise yourself and think, 'This is me all over, I know I can succeed' or were you a little more circumspect, and felt that some of the qualities you had, and others were yet to fully flourish.

Before you move forward in the book, take some time to reflect on how you compare with the seven essential qualities. We are so busy day to day that we can neglect to think about our internal workings, and what drives us. You have spent some time on this already with the values work in Chapter 1, now it's time to consider your behavioural tendencies and how they will support you as you move forward in starting your business.

Remember, owning your own business is like an intense never-ending personal development course. Consider these exercises the pre-work.

From my experience coaching over the last decade, in both large multinationals and with micro-business owners, I know that when we are discussing intangible soft skills in business it helps to get very specific about them. The more tangible we make these skills, the easier it is to build them to where you need to be.

When we are aware of something it is much easier to understand it, and then change it if we want to. How we work internally is no different. The first place to start is to give yourself a measure. This will provide a benchmark to move from.

Using the following Corporate Crossover Essential Qualities Wheel, rate yourself out of ten on each quality.

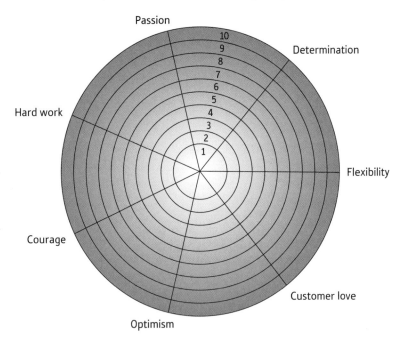

Once you have completed the wheel, reflect on the pattern you see.

- What areas are you strongest at?
- Where could you develop some more?

You will probably have a naturally strong tendency in three to four areas. And that is a great foundation to start from.

Use the following Worksheet to think more about what you need to do, to shift the scores to where you would like them.

Enhancing your success qualities

1. **Passion**

   How much do you exhibit this quality? Score ___/10

   Give an example of you using it.

   What score would you like to grow to? Score ___/10

   What could you do differently to increase your score? (For example, speak with your end user, think about and write down the differences it could make if you increase your score, write down what you love and why, etc.)

2. **Determination**

   How much do you exhibit this quality? Score ___/10

   Give an example of you using it.

   What score would you like to grow to? Score ___/10

   What could you do differently to increase your score? (For example, think about the difference a success will make, break your big goal into smaller steps to make it easier to achieve, etc.)

3. **Optimism**

   How much do you exhibit this quality? Score ___/10

   Give an example of you using it.

   What score would you like to grow to? Score ___/10

What could you do differently to increase your score? (For example, write down three things that went well each day, look for the positive in each situation, etc.)

4. **Customer love**

   How much do you exhibit this quality? Score ___ /10

   Give an example of you using it.

   What score would you like to grow to? Score ___ /10

   What could you do differently to increase your score? (For example, speak with your customers and write down ideas for ways to delight them, etc.)

5. **Courage**

   How much do you exhibit this quality? Score ___ /10

   Give an example of you using it.

   What score would you like to grow to? Score ___ /10

   What could you do differently to increase your score? (For example, practise being bold on less important things, enrol on a confidence-building course involving ropes and heights, etc.)

6. **Flexibility**

   How much do you exhibit this quality? Score ___ /10

   Give an example of you using it.

   What score would you like to grow to? Score ___ /10

   What could you do differently to increase your score? (For example, taking action following feedback, asking more people for their opinions, etc.)

7. **Hard work**

How much do you exhibit this quality? Score ___ /10

Give an example of you using it.

What score would you like to grow to? Score ___ /10

What could you do differently to increase your score? (For example, set regular working hours, agree deadlines and meet them, etc.)

Be savvy

Remember we never stay static. We are constantly evolving. So if you have completed these exercises and feel as if you don't have what it takes but you still really want to start your business then you can learn and acquire these attributes.

If you are feeling doubtful about your ability to learn then cast your mind back to when you learnt a new skill ... this is no different and entirely possible if you want it.

Caution

It's easy in this part to be paralysed by introspection and comparison to unrealistic ideals of successful entrepreneurs presented by the media. Instead of focusing on what is different about you compared to 'Famous Household Name' entrepreneur – focus on what's similar.

Busy woman's shortcut

Don't waste time with self-doubt. If you're feeling anxious and low, try not to dwell on it. Instead, tell yourself that you just need to tick one thing off your list. Often just achieving one thing will propel you forward to get cracking with the rest of the list and start feeling good about yourself. In essence – stop worrying and start doing!

Chapter

What are my aspirations?

Time to shift your thinking up a gear. You know you want a business, and you have the beginning of an idea, which over the next few chapters will become more refined as your confidence and commitment grow.

Before we get into the detail of starting to create the plan for your business, let's lift your thinking to what your dream for this business is.

By the end of this chapter you will discover:

- why a vision for your business is essential
- how to create your own vision that you will love and will inspire you.

When you think of your business, where do you see it in five years' time? What will the business feel like and how will it impact your life?

An evocative and compelling business vision is key to your success. It will drive your passion. Passion underpins so many qualities of a successful business owner.

When you are starting up your business, visions capture your dreams, your hopes and the impact you want to make. They can give you a surge of pride, energy and excitement when you consider what it will be like to achieve this amazing vision you have created.

The business vision will enable you to see past the day to day detail and remind you of what the business is here to do, and how it will feel when that's achieved. It will become a motivating artefact, which you will return to again and again for that burst of inspiration and motivation.

In his speech to the joint session of Congress in 1961, President John F. Kennedy challenged the American space mission to get a man on the moon by the end of the decade, to beat the Russians. He said, 'I believe that this nation should commit itself to achieving the goal, before this decade is out, of landing a man on the moon and returning him safely to Earth.' He went on to say, 'If we were to go only half way or reduce our sights in the face of difficulty, it would be better not to go at all.'

In this famous speech, Kennedy galvanises and leads America into a new era in its space mission. He transcends the possible and predicted by setting an audacious target.

He harnessed the hearts and minds of all that worked on the project. Their dreams were realised on 21 July 1969 when Neil Armstrong became the first man to set foot on the moon, stepping onto the moon's surface into the Sea of Tranquility. Making the impossible possible.

In business, a compelling vision can have the same impact. A business vision has the following qualities:

- It paints the future of what we want to achieve.
- It represents both the audacious and realistic possibilities.
- It captures the dreams and hopes of those involved.
- It evokes a strong positive energy.

Having this vision will help you as you create the other aspects of your business plan. Beyond boosting your flagging spirits, a compelling vision will help you in the future as you start to make decisions that may have far-reaching consequences.

For instance, if you are choosing between two suppliers, which one will help you reach your vision, or shares the same values as you?

Creating a vision for your business

To create a vision for your business, start with a vision board. I love vision boards and have always used them as part of my planning. Vision boards are an effective tool to use as you create a new business, or even as you do your annual planning.

Even though I have used vision boards for years, I never really thought about how or why they worked, I just believed they did. Recently I had an experience that gave me cause to stop and reflect on their impact.

Unfortunately, my father died very suddenly in New Zealand and I flew from London for the funeral and to be with my family. I ended up being away for much longer than planned, and after packing his house up and getting it ready for sale, I returned to London.

Coming back to work (my own business) was really hard. Not only was I miserable and grieving, I felt dislocated from my normal life in the UK. As a coach and mentor I am supposed to motivate others and help them achieve goals but now the last thing I felt like doing was that, or even doing it to myself.

Then it clicked ... what tool in my tool box can I use to boost my flagging spirits and help me recapture energy and motivation to do what I know I really want to be doing?

It was, of course, my vision board. That personal and inspirational collection of images, words and colours, that when I created it six months ago defined where I wanted to go. Before all of the grief, every time I looked at it, I felt uplifted, on purpose and ready to get going on the next task at hand! This gave me the bursts of energy I needed.

From a neuroscience perspective, vision boards work as follows:

- When you are creating it and choose images that 'feel' right, you are accessing your subconscious. The subconscious drives your thinking most of the time.

- Your vision board makes you feel different. You feel happier, motivated, inspired. When you feel these emotions you are releasing a burst of oxytocin and dopamine into your brain – 'feel good' neuropeptides. These will help to energise you and get you into action.

- Looking at the vision board focuses your thinking. What you think you become... or in a more expanded way – what you think impacts your feelings. What you feel impacts what you do and what you do impacts your results. So by thinking about your board and lifting your feelings, this will help you take those actions you know you need to if you are to achieve the aspects of your vision board.

- Each time you look at the board you are creating new neural pathways – this means you are creating a different way of thinking about your future and desires. This new way of thinking helps you to learn and to take new actions.

- By imprinting the vision board on your brain (by looking at it frequently) you will start to unconsciously become more aware of opportunities, connections and conversations that will help you achieve your vision board. This is called reticular activation – you have probably experienced this already if you have ever made a decision to buy a specific model car and then suddenly started seeing it everywhere. This isn't because they suddenly started making more of them, but rather you have subconsciously started to become more aware of them because you made the decision to buy one. Imagine if you had this subconscious help to achieve your vision!

Vision boards are an essential and effective tool as you begin your new business. They also help you define more fully what your business is to be. The examples of vision boards below are ones I have created at different phases over the ten years I have had my business. As you can see, my thinking has evolved over that time!

A few years ago I had a woman in my workshops who had recently left her job in banking. Her business idea was to start a wellbeing and fitness service targeting male executives who worked in the City. When she completed her vision board, the images she had selected were very feminine and centred on women's fitness and wellbeing. My client was shocked. This exercise helped her to realise that after many years in a male-dominated environment, she had lost sight of her femininity. She realised that she wanted to work with women, and then shifted her proposition to reflect that. Just 18 months later she has launched a fantastic range of fitness clothing for women.

 Create a vision board

Have some fun with this one ... it's your time to dream and imagine!

Create a vision board of what you would like your business to be like. Take some time out – grab your favourite magazines and a pair of scissors. Imagine what your business will be like, what you want to achieve, how you want your business to be.

Leaf through the magazine and cut out any picture, word or image that attracts you. You may not understand what it represents but if it speaks to you – GRAB IT!! Then stick these onto a sheet of paper and voila! Your vision board for your business!

As you think about where you want your business to be in five years' time, it might be helpful to keep in mind the following:

- Who are your customers?
- What are you doing?
- Where are you doing it?
- What do you love about your work?
- What makes each day fantastic?

Making your business vision tangible

Now you have created the visual representation of where you want your business to be, you need to bring it into a more tangible form. Use the Worksheet below to reflect on the future you have created for your business and yourself on the vision board.

 Describe the business you want to create

Now you have your completed your vision board, write down what your business will be like when you have created it. Look at your vision board for inspiration and be as descriptive as you can. This is your chance to get your thoughts down on a piece of paper. If you need some help starting, consider the following:

- What will you be selling to your customers?
- What will they like about your business?
- Will you employ others, who will they be, what will they be like?
- What will your business look like (shop window, website, office, etc.)?

- What will your daily routine be like?
- How will this change your life?

Taking the time to reflect on it now will help you solidify your thoughts and musings. And by getting these onto a piece of paper, your dreams will change to become goals. This simple shift will make them all the more achievable.

When we have a single-minded target of what we want to achieve, it is much easier to make this happen. Our focus is laser sharp, and our energy is directed to achieve that goal.

In JFK's speech, his single-minded goal was to get a man on the moon before the end of the decade. It was a simple statement with one focus. An American on the moon before 1970.

JFK's mission could be termed a Big Hairy Audacious Goal. This wonderful term describes a goal so big, it seems completely mad to go after it, and in the same breath, so scary it makes your hairs stand up.

A Big Hairy Audacious Goal is compelling, evocative and inspirational. It will be a statement that your future team will rally behind, a goal that your suppliers will want to partner with you to make happen and a goal that will give you immense pleasure when you progress towards it.

Here are two Big Hairy Audacious Goals from the women business owners I spoke to writing this book:

Sandra Roycroft-Davies has a very evocative vision for her Thinking Slimmer business: 'To be bigger than Weight Watchers in ten years.'

Jessica Butcher of Blippar: 'To see Blippar become a commonly used, everyday verb – to 'blipp''. This would mean that Blippar had reached the same behavioural take up as Twitter – to tweet and Google – I will google it.'

 ## What is your Big Hairy Audacious Goal for your business?

Create your Big Hairy Audacious Goal for your business. Here are some examples from my past clients:

- To positively impact the health of the UK.

- To have clients from all over the world.

- To work three days a week and earn more than in my last job.

Take your wonderful vision board, and put it somewhere you will see it every day: in your office, your kitchen, wherever you will be working. Seeing it every day will remind you of the amazing business you wish to create.

Also make a big copy of your Big Hairy Audacious Goal and stick that right beside your vision board. Together these will work to inspire you as you continue through your journey.

Busy woman's shortcut

This can be an easy exercise to put off as you may feel it's too creative, too dreamy or ‹insert your excuse here›. Vision boards are a fantastic tool to enable you to think big, so make the time to do it.

I find it helps to do it with a friend. Take an evening out, each bring magazines and maybe a bottle of wine. Put on some nice music, light a candle and start! Doing it with someone else gives you the support and makes it a lovely experience.

Caution

Go for progress not perfection. It can be tempting to get caught in the trap of wanting the perfect vision board with just the right images. If you are wanting this, then your logical mind is driving the process, not your intuitive mind. Let go, and trust that whatever magazines you have, the images you find will be the right ones.

Be savvy

Take this time to DREAM and IMAGINE! Create an evocative future of your business and your life. There is plenty of time later to be concerned with the nuts and bolts of making the business a reality. Think big, reach high and trust that you will create the best version of your future business.

Part

Is my idea right for the market?

Once an idea is formed and you are committed to beginning a business, it is imperative that you ensure a market exists for your offering, and that people will buy it. This will give you more confidence your business will be a success.

As you work through the following chapters, you will begin a voyage of discovery. I will encourage you to look at market information, get up close and personal with your ideal customers and throughout all of this be constantly refining your idea.

It is very rare to create the perfect saleable idea in the first instance. Most often, the idea is refined as you continue to get feedback, understand more about the market place and develop a deeper knowledge about your offering and the type of business you wish to create.

All the Worksheets are available at **www.CorporateCrossovers. com/MyNewBusiness**, so take some time to download and work through them as you go through this part. And remember, now is the time to keep learning and refining, so that when you do launch you have the best possible offering available.

By the end of this part, you will know exactly what you are selling and who will buy it. This may sound like an obvious thing to do but so often I have coached business owners who are not specific about this. Therefore they find it hard to position themselves against the competition and to succinctly and specifically explain what they are selling to whom.

I want you to get clear on what you are proposing. By the end of the following four chapters you will bring all of your thinking, research, feedback and ideas together and crystallise them into a value proposition.

The value proposition is a simple way to explain the following:

- what you are selling

- who will buy it and why

- how you stand out from the competition

- why your customer will come back for more.

Value propositions distil your offering into a specific and succinct statement, so you can clearly and easily articulate what your business is. It is designed around your target customer, so you will know what value you are giving them when they buy your offering.

 Your value proposition

When you have worked through this part, download and complete the following Worksheet:

My (insert your target customer):

will choose (insert your product/service):

to help with (insert the pain/problem):

ahead of the competition (insert what makes you different from the competition):

they will return for more because (insert how they benefit from buying from you):

The value proposition will become a foundation piece for your business. You will use it to describe your business to those people who will help you create your business presence: your web designer, brand designer, employees, freelancers, ad agency, etc.

The value proposition you create now will change and improve as you acquire new knowledge, not only from this book and the related work you do, but also from the market place, your suppliers, your retailers etc. and this will all be added into the mix to make your plan as robust as possible.

Creating a great value proposition

The easiest way to create a value proposition is to create it step by step. Walk through each chapter in this part to get the information you need. In the last chapter of this part, you will bring it all together.

 ### What am I selling?

The easiest place to start is with what you are selling. Before you start completing the work to create the value proposition, take some time to write down exactly what you plan to sell. The discipline of writing the description down will take your thinking to another level, by getting it out of your head and onto a piece of paper. And with all of the additional work you have done since you started reading this book, it may have shifted slightly!

An easy way to do this is to imagine you are telling your best friend exactly what you are planning to sell. How would you describe it to them?

If you are selling a product, describe exactly what the product is. For instance, if you are creating and selling jewellery, a description might be, I am selling hand-made necklaces and earrings using precious gems and gold and silver. Or if you have a service, maybe you are selling advice and information to landlords via courses, books, webinars, online learning etc.

Write down what you are selling now.

5

Is there a market for it?

As you learn more about your offering and your market, your passion and enthusiasm will increase, as the intangible starts to become tangible. You begin to feel more confident about beginning the business.

This chapter will encourage you to do some fact finding about the space you are about to enter. You will be able to:

- identify if a market already exists and how vibrant it is
- discover the key metrics of the market, which will help in your decision making.

Does a market exist for my idea?

So now you have a vision you are getting excited about the tantalising possibilities that your new business represents. You enter an exciting phase as you start to envisage your bright, new future.

To enhance your confidence about your idea, we need to do more fact finding. When we are analysing whether or not we should take our business concept to the next level, it is imperative that we know whether or not a market exists for our idea.

All the great visioning in the world, and your intense passion, is a waste of time and energy if there is no market that will buy it. Whilst you may be eager to get started and launch, taking the time to investigate will pay dividends.

This research will enable you to speak more confidently about:

- your market
- how your market is composed
- key trends
- competitors, etc.

This knowledge will enable you to make better-informed decisions. You can have more rigorous conversations with suppliers, distributors, customers, the press and potential investors.

You probably have a hunch whether or not a market exists, but if you want to pitch your business plan for investment, either with a venture capitalist or a bank, you are going to need to quantify the market opportunity for them.

Investigating and understanding the market you want to enter is very important. This research will provide you with more insight and knowledge and you will start to understand if the market is vibrant and growing, or whether it has hit the doldrums and is in its last dying stages.

Whatever you discover, it will give you pause for thought. A chance to check in and make sure this is an idea worth pursuing, or not. All of these facts will help you make informed, objective decisions about something that will have a significant impact on your life.

The trick with this piece of research is to give it a light touch, and not get bogged down in reports or lose yourself in the black time hole of googling. You need to go in with a sharp focus, get the information you need, and then move on.

It's a good idea to conduct the market analysis in steps:

- Step 1: Describe your market
- Step 2: How big is your market?
- Step 3: Market changes

Step 1: Describe your market

Quite simply, you need to define which market you are going to operate in. Be as specific as possible. Imagine if I had a luxury aromatherapy skincare range that I wanted to launch – think Jo Malone but with the therapeutic benefits of aromatherapy – I could say that my market was the UK skincare industry, but that is far too broad and meaningless. If I were to define it like this, I would be comparing myself with Vaseline and Dove, and really, they are not my key competition, so that is not going to be very helpful. Furthermore, the thought of going up against the market giants is intimidating.

But if I was to define my market as the UK aromatherapy skincare market, or the UK luxury skincare market, then I would gain a much more precise understanding of this sector. I would be competing against brands including Tisserand, Eve Taylor and Balance Me.

This specificity will allow you to get a better knowledge of a small section of the market faster. It will also come in handy when you are analysing your competition. By defining the market you plan to enter so much more tightly will help you find data, trends, insights and get a very good understanding of what is happening in that specific niche.

When Helen Pattinson of Montezuma's returned from South America she spent a lot of time in the British Library researching her new-found passion – chocolate. She recalls: *'I spent days and days in there because the internet was still in its infancy and it was much harder to get hold of decent market research. I had access to all the Mintel market research reports as I wanted to work out what the chocolate industry was like in this country.'*

Helen was focused in her research, as she wanted to discover if there were any gaps in the UK market that they could launch into: *'We were looking to see if there was a gap in the market. It was quite a pointed effort to discover the whole industry before we made our leap. The striking thing was that there were no small chocolate companies. That's how we decided to make our business, in the small independent sector.'*

Describe your market

Define the market place in which you will be operating. Try to be as specific as possible, narrow your field down from the industry (e.g. UK skincare) to the sector (e.g. UK aromatherapy skincare). This will give you a much deeper understanding of the market dynamics and enable you to size your opportunity more accurately.

Step 2: How big is your market?

Knowing the size of the market that you are entering will help you quantify the opportunity and potential for you and your business. If you are going after funding, then again, this will be an essential piece of information. The investor will be interested in how much growth they can expect from you and the market, and they will use this to work out their return on investment.

The market size can be measured in two ways, the number of units sold and the sales value (turnover) of the market. Other useful statistics about the market size can include:

- the market value – how much money is represented by the market place
- market metrics:
  - number of units sold
  - number of businesses
  - number of employees
  - number of customers (especially if business to business)

Select whatever market metrics are most relevant to you. There are many places where you can buy reports on sizes of markets or you can do your own desk research through the internet. The British Library and the City Guildhall Library are also fantastic places to find this data. Look at company reports, industry magazines, FT.com and journals (*The Economist, Investors' Chronicle*, etc.) – see also the resources at the end of the chapter. These will all have information on market trends and sizes, and companies that are in your space. Collecting this type of information will make you more informed about the area you are starting your business in. With more information, you can make better-informed decisions and increase your likelihood of success.

You may be thinking that you are too busy to do this research. And I know you are busy. But it's not just the market size you will discover by doing this investigation – lots of other interesting facts and figures will come into your field of view. These will spark off new ideas for your business, you will learn what's worked and hasn't for your competition, and you will start to grow your intuitive feel for the market.

Below is an example of how a market can be sized:

I want to start a landscaping business for homes. From the Mintel online report (at http://store.mintel.com/) I gathered the following information about the landscaping business in the UK:

- It's worth £4 billion.
- It grew by 4.6 per cent last year.
- It employs 60,000 people.
- There are 15,600 businesses.

This tells me that this industry is growing faster than the economy, which would suggest it is quite buoyant.

The above example shows a broad-brush look at an entire industry. If I was to be much more specific (for example, if my business idea was to open a landscaping business for home owners in Devon), then I would want to drill down deeper into the numbers and get a feeling for the size nationally of domestic landscape gardeners, and then drill down again into specific geographical locations.

If you don't want to pay for a report, or your library doesn't have it, then you need to estimate the market size yourself. Use Google, your hunches and your imagination.

Using the example above of landscaping residential properties in Devon, I would do a local search on Google, and list as many local companies as possible. For example here are some I made up for my landscaping example:

- Paradise Landscaping
- Absolute Landscaping
- Graham Gardens
- Trees and Trellis
- Sanctuary Creations

You will need to research what the sales turnovers are for each business. If you go to Companies House, this will give you the company accounts, which are available for public view. You can then easily see what the sales turnover for the past trading year has been. (This is also a useful piece of information when it comes to estimating your turnover for your first year of trading.)

By creating your own market place from all these businesses you find, and then adding up their turnovers, you will have a market size estimate relevant to your specific sector.

Also, while you are doing your research, try to get the historical data. This will help you know if the market is shrinking or expanding and give you a feel for which businesses are doing well, and which aren't. This detail will give you a great understanding of the market place you will be entering. You will see who your competition is, what they offer and how they talk about their products or services.

Useful websites for market information:

- www.cityoflondon.gov.uk
- www.bl.uk/bipc/
- http://store.mintel.com/
- http://www.reportlinker.com
- http://www.ibisworld.co.uk
- http://www.marketresearch.com
- http://www.research-insight.com

How big is your market?

Knowing the size of the market that you are entering will help you quantify the opportunity and potential for you and your business. If you are going after funding, then this is an essential piece of information. Note down which metrics are most relevant to you and your business.

You need to consider:

- the value of the market – how much is sold in that market place each year
- the volume of the market – units sold, number of businesses, number of customers, etc.

Step 3: Market changes

How is the market changing? Is the market growing, shrinking, being besieged by political interference or riding the new wave of popularity?

Discover what is happening in your market place. When you are doing your research, keep an eye out for insights, trends, forecasts, and signs of growth or shrinkage. Also think about what the market may be missing. Is there a gap that has yet to be filled?

It is important that you have a view on where the market will be in the next 12 months and five years so you have a sense of the medium- to long-term viability of your idea.

When you are considering other influences on your market, consider:

- income growth
- political changes and their impact
- environmental changes
- population growth
- social factors
- technological factors
- society trends.

Also, consider what the risk factors will be, which could stall the growth completely.

Anna Bastek, co-founder and Marketing Director at Wolfestone, created a full service translation and localisation company. Working with over 6,000 translators globally, her clients include BBC, Mercedes, NATO and Coca Cola. She wanted to create a scalable business in a high growth market. *'I was looking at many different opportunities but the translation industry was growing strongly because of globalisation and increasing exports. From my research I discovered it was growing quickly at 8% per year. In addition, I discovered that a lot of competitors didn't put much effort into marketing and that was my strength. I knew I could make a difference by focusing on what customers really wanted and communicating this message clearly. In the long run this has led us to adding several complimentary services such as multilingual SEO, voice-overs, subtitling and desktop publishing. This has helped us win hundreds of international clients.'* Anna's research gave her the confidence to create a business in a market that she had no experience in.

Be savvy

As you are going through the research, be sure to pick out the juicy titbits that could give you good ideas, contacts, sales leads and other useful pointers for your new business. That way, you don't have to trawl through all of the information again.

Caution

Being part of the first dot-com explosion, I saw a lot of PowerPoint presentations by eager entrepreneurs who all insisted their idea would be the one that would get the 1 or 2 per cent of the market, and riches and fame would be plentiful. Market size is one way to estimate the scope of your business but you also need to consider other factors as well.

WOW, if the market is worth £4 billion and I get one per cent of it, that means I will get £40 million. If only it were that simple...

Busy woman's shortcut

In my early years as a marketing manager for Colgate toothpaste (way before the internet – I think the fax machine had just been invented!), we would be given mammoth red folders, weighing at least 4 kilos, of pages full of numbers. Once a month these tomes would be delivered, with every piece of data imaginable about what size tube of toothpaste, in all the many flavours and variants, sold in what supermarket across the country, at what price. Did I need to know this to make a strategic decision on how to improve my advertising message or know what my competitors were up to? No I didn't – I just needed the top-line information to stay informed and up to date.

And really, that's all you need to do here – otherwise you could find yourself swimming in a big black hole of information overload! Avoid the risk of procrastination and getting struck by paralysis by analysis.

Chapter

Who are my competitors and how can I be different?

Is your idea completely original, or is it a copy or an improvement of something else already existing in the market? Wouldn't it be amazing if we knew that our product was completely different, the market space we will enter was vibrant and we had no competition?

By the end of this chapter you will discover:

- who your competition is
- how it feels to be one of their customers
- what needs to be refined about your idea based on your new knowledge.

To ensure your business idea is a success, you need to know:

- Is it different to what else is out there?
- Not only is it different, but also how is it better?
- What qualities does it have that will ensure your prospect selects you over your competition?

When I am teaching this part of the Start Your Own Business Programme (a virtual course I created and lead with Mumsnet and Pearson College), my participants start to shrink away as fear floods their minds. They fear looking at their competition. It's as if they think by studying them closely, they will become intimidated by what is already in the market, and become discouraged to launch. It is quite normal to feel threatened by our competitors.

But this fear or intimidation will get you nowhere. It can consume you and disempower you from taking those bold steps you need to take to get your business started. I have learnt in over ten years of running my own business, and before that when I worked in corporates, that competition is a great thing. Here's why:

1. **Proof a market exists.** If you have competition in your space, it means that there is a market. It confirms you are not crazy and thinking there is an opportunity when one doesn't really exist. You can rest easy at night knowing that someone else has forged a path ahead of you. They also help you build a market if you are entering a new space.

2. **Competition keeps you fresh.** Having competition keeps you sharp. To enter the market successfully you need to be better and different to what is already out there. You can learn so much from what your competition does well, and where they could do better. This curiosity will help you refine your offering and market presence. Over the years, I have learnt not to be intimidated or scared of my competition but instead to be curious and wonder what I can learn to improve my business.

As Sun-Tzu said, 'Keep your friends close, and your enemies closer'.

When you were investigating the market in the previous chapter, you probably started to discover more about your competition.

To really benefit from their presence in the market, I want you to get even more intimate with them. Knowing and reflecting on how they talk about their offering, who their ideal customer is, and how and where they sell, will give you solid information about how to create your own business.

For instance, if you are wondering how you will get your high-end jewellery product sold, studying how other jewellery companies in your segment do this will give you some great ideas. They have already completed the hard work of setting up and creating their brand, website, finding suppliers and making their product. Put your curiosity hat on, and see this as an easy way to learn about building your own business, not a fearful undertaking.

Jane of Jane Plan, the diet delivery service, assessed the market before she launched her business. She went and bought her competitors' food to try it out: *'I thought I'm going to try all these plans out, and what I found was that some were very, very good but very, very expensive. Some were not very good and I thought, "There's got to be something in the middle here where you can buy something that's very, very good but at a price that is accessible for most people"'*. Jane knows that she didn't invent the idea but as she says: *'Jane Plan is a unique take on an idea that already existed. I wanted something that was really good food, readily accessible but most importantly created in a very supportive environment for anyone who decides to embark on the plan.'*

Learning about your competition

Step 1: Be a customer (experiential research)

So, how do you get to know your competition? Simple, become a customer. As odd as that may sound, I want you to pretend you are one of their prospective customers and then experience what it is like to search for, buy and use their product. Imagine you are a mystery shopper. How do they greet you, how is the product or service delivered, what is their customer service like?

Taking the time to review your competitors objectively and to learn from them will give you more confidence as you start to grow your business. It will also help you shape your marketing message later on.

As you go through their customer journey, always ask yourself:

- What is great about what they offer?
- How do you think your prospect would like it?
- What could they do better?
- Would I use them again?

Take some time to think about all the things they are doing well – whether that is packaging, price point, easy to use website, helpful and friendly customer service on the phone. Do get into the detail and reflect on what it means to you and your business idea. Use the following Worksheet to record your experience as a customer of your competition.

Catherine Watkin, creator of Selling from the Heart, a sales mentoring company, had experienced other sales training companies and knew exactly what she didn't want to be like: '*I know what sales training is like, I've been through loads of it myself, it doesn't excite me. I find a lot of it manipulative, and most of the tools they gave you, I never used myself.*' But she realised that she could offer something very different and in alignment with her values: '*I sell with integrity and authenticity. I came across this phrase "heart centred" online somewhere, and I thought, "That's me, that's what I am, heart-centred sales". I then ran a one-day workshop from this basis.*' That was the start of Catherine's very successful business.

Customer experience with your competitors

- What is great about what they offer?
- How do you think your prospect would like it?
- What could they do better?
- Would you use them again?
- How did you feel as a customer?

Step 2: Analyse their offer (desk research)

Now you have experienced what it is like to be a customer, take the analysis deeper to understand how they present their offer. Remember how all of this knowledge goes into your bones and will enhance your 'gut feel' in the future.

Detailed competitive analysis

Select five competitors and analyse them against the criteria by doing the Worksheet below.

You want to discover:

- What is the problem they are solving for their customer?
- How do they talk about their offering?
- Why do their customers love them?
- How long have they been in the market?
- What is their market presence (or market share if you have that)?
- How well known are they?
- How are they priced (high, low, premium, etc.)?
- Where do they source their goods from?
- How to they sell in the market place?
- Who is their typical customer?
- What is their vision?
- How do they operate? How many staff, location, online and offline presence, sales force etc.?

Answering what you can of these 12 questions will give you an in-depth understanding of who you are competing against and importantly, what your prospect has to choose from.

How do you compare?

You have completed some great work to discover more about the other entrants in your space. It's time to bring this fact finding together and see how you compare.

Remember you are still in the refining stage of your idea. Making changes now is easy and low cost compared to when you have launched and spent considerable amounts of time, energy and money. So treat this next step as a bonus gift, saving you from an expensive rework of your offering later on.

Refining your idea

To refine your idea against your newly gained knowledge of the market place and the competitors, work though these questions.

1. Overall how do you compare to what is out there in the market?

2. What do you think your idea will do better than the competition?

3. Based on what you have seen, what needs to change to be even better?

4. What have you loved the most about all that you have seen?

5. What do you think customers love the most about the competition?

6. Why would they buy again from the competition?

7. What might make customers stop buying from their current provider, and choose you?

8. Typically, how does your competition tell prospects about their offering?

9. List the ten key insights you have learnt from diving deep and studying the competition.

Tracy Mort, founder and MD of Grace Cole, knows her early success was due to her market knowledge: *'I knew my market place and I knew my product, I knew the price it needed to retail at. You don't have to have launched to know that.'* She goes on to say: *'You need to be aware of your competitors. Don't be afraid of them, be aware of them. It's really, really important that you know your market place, you have to know where you're going to go and what you are going to sell. You have to know what your customers want.'*

Busy woman's shortcut

If all of this experiential research feels like it will take up a lot of time, then enlist help! Get a list of your competition and divide up the research between friends. Then you can meet up and compare notes. The great thing about this is that as well as saving time, you will get a much broader perspective than just your own.

Be savvy

When I first started coaching in Tokyo, there were two English-speaking coaches. Upon leaving two years later, there were ten. I know that meant I had five times as many competitors, but I also had five times as many people speaking about coaching. They were helping educate the market about the benefits of being coached. This really helped my business grow, as I didn't need to search so hard for people who knew what coaching was and were considering it.

Caution

It can be easy to feel overwhelmed and discouraged when you are researching the competition. Try to avoid this. Remember there is always room in the market for more than one type of anything. People love a choice, Think about how many different cars there are, models of phones, styles of backpack, even holiday options. The key to thinking about your opportunity in the face of competition is to be very clear on the problems you are solving for your target customer.

Who are my customers and what do they think?

The market is looking vibrant, and you know you can stand out from the competition. Your confidence that you have a viable idea is growing. Things are certainly moving in the right direction. You have done a lot of work to get this far, and I want to acknowledge you for that.

The next part of developing your new business is to get up close and personal with your ideal customer. By the end of this chapter you will discover:

- how to create a vivid description of your ideal customer
- what their problems are that you can solve
- how to conduct research to gain confidence that your idea will work.

Having a unique idea in a growing market is one part of the equation. The other piece is having someone to sell to. I know this sounds obvious when you read it, but I have worked with, unfortunately, too many business owners who haven't really considered this. So they have a fantastic website, bright shiny new business cards and leaflets, and they can't understand why no one is buying what they have to sell.

Quite simply, they neglected taking the time to understand who their prospective customer was and what they needed.

The more intimate you are with your desired customer, the more easily you will be able to:

- Solve their problems.
- Talk to them in a language that resonates with them.
- Display information about your offering in places where they will see it.
- Deliver the experience in a way you know they will love, and hopefully come back for more.

To be able to match your customers' needs, you need to know the language they use and how they gather information about new products and services. You need to imagine the world from their perspective. Get into their shoes, live a day in their life, think about what they would buy, read, view on the web. It's time to put your imagination to work.

When you are razor sharp on exactly who you are selling to it will make your job much easier in the future. You will know what your marketing message needs to be to appeal to them, you will know how to price it, and importantly, how to reach them with your marketing activity.

> Cleopatra from Celtic Quest Coasteering recalls the difference being specific in her target market made to the business: 'Nailing the target market was key for the business because initially there was a scatter-gun approach. We'll take anyone, anybody please. Whereas now we are pickier about who we like to take out. We have moved from hung-over bachelor parties to families in the AB demographic. With this move we also priced ourselves out of the cheap stag market, and now we are reassuringly high and this seems to attract more mums.'

Getting intimate with your customer is key because I believe our greatest competitor is not actually the other entrants in the market, but our own inertia. How often do you think you 'should' do something, or buy that service you heard about, or try out that new product or even change brands of washing detergent but you do nothing about it? What will it take to move someone from not being interested and doing nothing, to buying?

I know from my own experience it is when I feel that someone, whether face to face, on a web page or an ad, is talking to me specifically, as if they have read my mind. From what they say, or what is written, they identify with my pains and problems. They may have even had those issues themselves and they have a solution that will solve them!

Really getting into your customers' heads is the key to this. So, you need to imagine who they are and what keeps them awake at night. The more you know about them, the easier it is to sell to them.

I never stop learning about my customers. I am always meeting my target market at networking events, following them on social media, reading their blogs, and of course I do research. Keeping my customers and their needs at the top of my mind helps me to create products and services I know they need and will want to buy.

Create a detailed picture of your ideal customer

Take an individual from your prospect group and imagine who they are, what their life is like, where they live, what they do.

This may seem a little strange, but by being so detailed and descriptive, it will help you to craft your offerings and message to meet their needs. Before you go any further, I can already hear the protests firing off in your head. The two main objections you will be having are:

1. How on earth can I find so much detail? I have no idea! Well if that's what you think at this early stage – then give up now.

Because if you can't imagine what your customers' lives are like, then you will not be able to imagine what problems they need to solve, and how you will be able to solve them and get paid for it.

2. By singling out just one person means that I miss out on all the other people that might buy my offering. Yes, I can see how you will think that. Tightly defining one individual in your prospect community does not mean that you are excluding the rest of them. By deeply understanding them it means that you can much more easily craft and refine your offering and your message. Start at the start and go with the person who you think would most closely represent the greatest number of your ideal client base.

Kay White, savvy and influential communication expert for women in business and founder of Way Forward Solutions, experienced a large upswing in her business when she tightly defined her niche and offering. '*Originally I had an executive coaching organisation, Way Forward Coaching. This was focused on what you want in your career, what your next move is going to be, and then it evolved into workshops and leadership. Soon I got enough traction to really know that I could get results for women. They would get promoted, their team would start to respond to them, and they would have better relationships with their bosses. I became aware that in each case it was around how I had shown them how to express themselves. Realising that this is really what I am passionate about, and it's what I am good at, I decided to focus on women in business expressing themselves more effectively.*'

Kay goes on to tell of how narrowing in on that position helped her business: '*It became easier. I knew what I was focusing on and what I could leverage. I changed the shape of the business as well and went online. Consequently, it has exploded financially in comparison to where it was.*'

The more specific you are, the simpler it will be for people to understand what you offer and whether or not it is for them. The specificity of your prospect will also help you enormously when it comes to creating a marketing plan. The more you can imagine what they are like, the easier it is to come up with compelling ideas to entice them to buy.

Creating a detailed picture of your ideal client requires you to imagine:

- what their life is like
- what their problems and needs are related to your market place.

I have sketched out some examples below.

The ideal client of a business that provides advice to landlords could be described as follows:

- Her name is Jenny (I find it helps to name them).
- She is 42, and lives in north London. She has owned property since she started working in her early twenties and has got four flats she rents out.
- She works full time for a newspaper.
- She works long hours.
- She drives a VW Golf.
- She doesn't have kids, but lives with her partner.
- She likes to run at the weekend but is too busy to exercise during the week.
- She earns around £75,000.
- She likes to holiday in Europe.
- She also likes to go to the cinema and the theatre and entertain friends at home.

It is important to get this detail so you can imagine how your offering will fit into their life. Knowing what media they consume and how they spend their time will also help you plan your marketing activity. It also gives you a sense of how you need to interrupt their life, to make them aware of your services and move them from inertia.

The following is a real-life example of my ideal client for my business Corporate Crossovers®. I work with women who leave their jobs to set up their own businesses.

My ideal client is called Robyn:

- Robyn has a good job as a senior executive PA.
- She is fed up with the politics and the stress.
- In her spare time she designs jewellery and sells the pieces to her friends.
- She lives in west London.
- She is married with two kids.
- She has a dog, is responsible for the school run and the house.
- She takes the dog for a walk every day.
- She has no time for other hobbies or a social life.
- She drives a VW.

These details help me think carefully about how I would talk to and reach Robyn with my marketing message. She's busy working. She probably doesn't go out to networking groups but I would imagine she is on LinkedIn (probably looking for a new job), active on Pinterest looking at jewellery designs and may be considering a shop on Etsy. As you can see, I already have made up some plausible assumptions about where she might be spending her time online. This will help me when I need to reach her.

Natalie Haverstock, aka Miss Ballooniverse, knew where her target market would be to launch her new balloon theatre business. She remembers how it started: 'It was really easy because I did it in such a small way. I got invited to be at the Highgate Fair in London, which is a wonderful event in a beautiful part of London, exactly where I knew my target market would be. So I got some business cards printed and handed them out at the event and that was it, my phone started ringing.' Natalie now has a blossoming ballooning business, employing 11 other balloon artists.

The life of your ideal customer

Consider who your ideal customer is. Try answering the following questions about them:

- Where do they live?
- What do they do?
- How much money do they earn?
- What type of car do they drive?
- What hobbies do they enjoy?
- Do they travel?
- What other aspects make up the profile of the life of your prospect?

What are your customer's problems and pains?

Once you have painted a picture of your customer's life, it's time to imagine what keeps them awake at night. What are their needs and their problems that may be related to your market place and your offering?

This step is essential to successfully refine your idea to ensure it solves a problem and has relevance to your target.

Let's look at Jenny, the part-time landlord.

She worries about:

- whether she is getting the best return from her properties
- paying management fees – but she doesn't think she knows enough to do it herself
- whether she should sell up and buy elsewhere
- an argument that is brewing with a long-standing tenant
- one of the flats which needs a major renovation – she's not sure whether it is worth it
- whether she should quit her job and do this full time – but she is scared.

So, you can see how, when we know the demographics of our target market, we can then imagine what they think about and what keeps them awake.

This knowledge of their pains and problems will help you to create your product or service to closely meet their needs. And the closer you meet their needs, the more likely they are to buy.

Let's look at my ideal target, Robyn. What are her pains?

- She is fed up with her job and wants to make more jewellery.
- She knows a lot about creating jewellery and admin, but doesn't know anything about selling, finding retailers or making websites.
- She wants to make more money but doesn't know if she should sell direct or through shops.
- She worries if her business will be a success and cover her bills.
- She doesn't know how to start a business.

When I am designing programmes and marketing messages for women who want to start their own business, I think of Robyn and her pains. That helps me get into the mind of my prospect so I can be sure I am creating something relevant for her.

And yes, I know it's an educated guess, but being so specific is so much better than saying I want to sell to women aged 35–50 who want to run their own business. That is too broad and far too vague. And also, that is exactly what my competition do, and I need to stand out if I am to be successful.

Your ideal customer's problems

Consider who your ideal customer is and imagine:

- what problems they have
- what frustrates them
- what they worry about
- what keeps them awake at night.

Make notes on your findings.

Refining your idea

Now go back to your idea from Chapter 2 and take some time to refine it based on what you have discovered so far.

Researching your idea

Now you have clarity about your idea, you need to grow your confidence that it will be successful. Would a complete stranger part with their hard-earnt money for your idea?

Once you have the answer to this question, then you can start your business. Conducting market research doesn't have to be a huge undertaking. It is a great way to learn more about your prospect and what they think of your offering.

This market research will help you discover:

- what your prospect thinks of your idea
- how they choose items
- what issues they may have that need solving
- what they think of the competition.

The purpose of the research is two-fold:

1. to get to know your prospect more and understand how they buy
2. to discover if your idea appeals to them.

This is a great opportunity to continue getting up close and personal with your prospect. The information you acquire will also help you to refine your offering to be as attractive as possible to them.

I know you did some initial testing of your idea back in Chapter 2. Since then you have completed more investigations into your market and understand your prospect better. This will culminate in your value proposition. This research will go up a level, taking your refined thinking into the market place for some robust feedback.

If you are considering funding, you will need to have proof that your idea is viable. This type of research will start to give you that information.

Justine Roberts from Mumsnet is an advocate of research: '*You must do something which is really useful and fulfils a need. So make sure that there is demand out there for whatever it is you choose to do. Keep checking in with the audience. I think sometimes you can get wedded to an idea, whether or not it is what people want. So keep checking that it is what people want and are finding it useful.*'

How to approach market research

If the thought of conducting market research is daunting and you think you need to get YouGov or Ipsos-MORI involved – fear not! My approach to market research is simple and effective.

Walk through the six steps below:

1. Who do you want to speak to?
2. How could you reach them?
3. How many people do you want to speak to?
4. What questions do you want to ask?
5. How will you collate their responses?
6. What will you do with the information once you have it?

1 Who do you want to speak to?

To get the most relevant feedback on your idea you must ask your target prospect. Of course this will be the prospect you identified in Chapter 7.

2 How could you reach them?

Think about the easiest and most efficient way you could reach them. For instance:

- If your prospect group is young mums, do you need to find local NCT groups, or mother and baby classes? Could you offer to buy coffee and cake for the group while you talk to them about your new idea?

- If you are after men who work in the City, is there a networking group you could visit as a guest, and start to meet some of their members to discuss your idea?

- Do you have a business idea that targets people who visit the gym frequently? Then you could visit gyms and start a conversation with them, or ring up the gym manager and ask if you could put a survey in their newsletter or on their website.

You can connect with your prospects to get their feedback in a number of ways:

- Meet your prospects face to face and ask them.

- Run an online survey on www.surveymonkey.com and send an email out to your prospects, on social media or LinkedIn, inviting them to do the survey.

- Visit local networking groups and ask if you can present your idea for feedback.

- Print out copies of your survey and take them to different groups and ask people to complete them.

- Host an evening or a coffee morning with a group of prospects and start talking about your idea.

- Visit clubs or networking groups where you know you are likely to find your prospect.

- Ask your friends and family if they know anyone who fit the description of your prospect, and meet or call them.

- If you are targeting a specific type of business owner, then you could search for businesses of that type and phone them.

- If you know what interests your target group, search out relevant groups on LinkedIn, Facebook and Google+. These groups are easy to join, and you can post asking for help. It's also a great way to discover what your target is talking about!

3 How many people do you want to speak to?

If you want to have a response that is statistically significant, then you need to get over 100 responses. If your passion is discovering means, standard deviations and all that, then you will need to get to that level, to feel confident about the results.

Many people though don't need that level of detailed analysis to make a decision about whether to launch or how to refine their idea. It may be that getting responses from 40 people is enough. The more people you do get responses from, the more confident you can be in your answers.

Aim to get at least 20. And if you think this is hard getting 20 people just to answer some questions about your idea, then frankly, give up now as you will need to make more than 20 sales to have a viable business.

It may feel uncomfortable asking people for their opinion of your idea, I know that. You may feel as if you are being judged. Having your own business is a constant cycle of doing new things and being stretched every day. This may be the first of many new things you feel are stretching you. Get familiar with the feeling. If you are feeling discomfort about this it is because you are stretching out of your comfort zone. You are beginning to show your idea to the world.

4 What questions do you want to ask?

Start with broad questions about the market, then get specific about your idea.

Here are some questions that you could ask your prospects:

- When you are deciding to buy (insert your specific market sector here) what do you consider when you are choosing?
- What products/service providers do you normally choose from?
- Why do you prefer one brand/shop/product/service provider over another?
- What do you love about the brand/shop/product/service provider that you buy from now?
- What could they (brand/shop/product/service provider) do better?
- What do you think of (your idea)?
- What do you like about it?

- What could be improved?
- How much would you expect to pay?
- Would you buy it?

5 How will you collate their responses?

Before you start the research decide how you will capture the responses. If you are meeting people face to face, will you take notes in a pre-made questionnaire, or jot down responses in your notebook? If it's easier for you, maybe ask them if they would mind if you recorded their answers.

If you are doing it online using an online tool, then that will be much easier for you. Each tool will have an elegant way of collecting answers for you.

6 What will you do with the information once you have it?

Once you get all of this information, compile all of the answers by question. This can be easy to do in a Word document or Excel spreadsheet. Print off the answers and take time to reflect.

 ## What I learnt from the research

Consolidate your learning from the research process by answering the following questions:

- What did I learn that was new?
- How could I apply this to my thinking about my business idea?
- How will I compare to the competition from my prospect's perspective?
- How much will they pay?
- What do I need to change about my value proposition to make it as desirable as possible?
- Did I learn anything new to add to my competitor analysis or market information?
- Did anything surprise me?

What is your refined idea?

Now you have all of this wonderful information from those complete strangers, revisit the value proposition you completed in the last chapter. What needs to change? Creating a strong idea for your business will be an iterative process, so you will keep learning, adding, refining as you go!

Consider:

- How close were you in your estimation of your prospects' problems?
- Does your idea meet their needs and solve a real problem?
- Are they likely to buy it or stick with your competition?

 Review

Review your value proposition and make the changes you need to.

Busy woman's shortcut

Whenever you go out, be it to a networking event, or to a party, start talking about your idea. Engage in a conversation and listen for what people have to say. Let them share with you their thoughts on the market, any problems or frustrations they have. You may not want to share your idea specifically with them, but having the conversation will add to your knowledge bank.

Caution

It is worth the time to do the research, as I know from hard learning many years ago.

The one time I launched a product with no market research it bombed. Fact. A long time ago, I was marketing manager for Smirnoff Vodka in Australia. The most popular way to drink Smirnoff in bars was with orange juice. So, we (my marketing director and I) thought it would be a no-brainer to put the vodka and orange into a can, and sell it. We knew the target market, I

Continued

had created a compelling value proposition and the sales force loved the idea, so we launched. It looked amazing on the shelves in the shops, and that's where it stayed. On the shelves. Until six months later we had to buy back the stock, and destroy it. Apart from the few cans some friends of mine bought in pity.

Why? We had enough facts, we knew litres of that combination were sold in bars all over the country every weekend but it stalled in the shops. I learnt a HUGE lesson that year. Never, ever make assumptions about what people will or won't buy. You must ask.

When I reflect on that scenario, and trust me, I don't take that memory out for a walk very often, I realise that there was enormous pressure from management to make the product and sell it. The numbers looked great – the profit margin was high, and we all thought sales would come easily.

I realised that when you are considering launching a new product or business, the whole bundle needs to make sense, the product, packaging, the profitability and of course ensuring a market will buy it.

So this doesn't happen to you, I urge you to take some time and find out from your prospects, who will be complete strangers, if they would be willing to buy your offering!

Be savvy

I love social media for doing research. Before I set up my new business, Corporate Crossovers®, I created a short questionnaire (I recommend no more than 10 questions) on **www.surveymonkey. com**. The brilliant thing about survey monkey is that people can answer your questionnaire quickly online, press send, and hey presto, you have all of their answers automatically compiled. Once you have set up the survey, which is very easy, then you have a web address you link into your social media posts, and the respondent just clicks on that to do the survey. Easy!

Because you can make it anonymous, that can encourage more people to answer. I received 300 replies to my survey. I placed the link to it on LinkedIn and Twitter and was overwhelmed by the response.

What is the idea I want to move forward with?

You have done a lot of thinking about your target customer, their pains and how you will reach them. And you have thought about how you can stand out in the market place.

Now is your chance to bring it all together and to create your value proposition for the refined idea you want to move forward with. By the end of this chapter you should be able to complete the following:

My…

will choose…

to help with …

ahead of the competition…

they will return for more because…

By bringing together all of these elements, you will be able to see at a glance, what it is you are bringing to market and why it will be a success. It will also allow you to see where you need to make refinements and changes, because you will see how it comes together and whether or not it makes sense and sounds compelling. Remember, at this stage it is a work in progress – once you get it into market research, you will want to make some changes to make it really stand out.

By now you will have a detailed understanding of your prospect customer:

- who they are
- how they live their lives
- what problems they would pay for to have solved.

Critical to the success of your idea are:

- knowing what their problems are
- knowing how you will solve them
- communicating the solution in a compelling and relevant way.

You will already have completed a lot of the work in previous chapters, but remember to take a critical look at how you complete the steps to ensure your thinking is centred around the customer.

Step 1: What are you selling?

Write down exactly what you plan to sell.

Step 2: What will it do for your customer?

Describe the problem you are trying to solve, and the difference your product or service will make to those people who buy it. Remember, they are paying for your idea to solve a problem or need that they have.

Go back to the list of problems that you created in the last chapter.

- How is your idea solving any of those problems?

- Have you described your idea in a way that describes the solution, or problem they want to solve?

- Are you clear enough on which problems you will solve, and how?

- Do you think you have an idea that will appeal to the profile of the prospect that you have explored?

- Are you solving a real problem or is it a 'nice to have'?

Remember the example I gave of someone who buys a spade not actually wanting to buy a garden tool, but instead the solution they are looking for is how to make a hole?

Or if I am selling coaching services, I am not selling one hour on the phone to talk with someone about their business, rather I am selling a way to get more focused about their business, feel in control and create a plan to make more money. I know from my research, that feeling out of control, not making enough income and having no focus are the three most common problems for small business owners. So I drafted my coaching marketing message to meet those problems.

For example, in the landlord service we looked at in the previous chapter this could help Jenny:

- increase her knowledge of tenancy laws and requirements

- deal with her problem tenants

- develop the ability to take over managing the properties herself

- create a step-by-step plan to help her restructure the properties so she is more aware of their financial position (this will also help her determine if she can stop working).

Take your list of problems and beside each one, write down how your idea will solve it. It may be that you need to think creatively about what words you use, how you describe your solution. It will be easier for you to come back to listing out what your idea does, but this isn't what the customer is interested in. That is what YOU are interested in! To communicate this effectively, you need to think about how you are enabling a positive change in your end user. That is the solution and the difference your idea will make to them.

Remember this process is iterative, so you can go back and change things once you have more knowledge, pondered things or discussed it with others. There is no risk in making the changes now. I know from my experience that I rarely get this right first time, so enjoy taking the time to walk through it.

 ## The solutions I am offering

List all the problems and pains in the left-hand column. Then think about how your idea solves those problems. List each solution next to the pain it solves.

My customers' problems	How I solve them

Now you are thinking about the solutions you can offer to your prospects, how does this change your original idea? How can you refine your original idea and craft it to be more solution oriented?

Step 3: Who will you be selling to?

 To really make an impact with your customer, you need to know them really well and understand what their key needs are. The more you know about them, the easier it is to sell to them.

In Chapter 7 you thought about your prospects, imagining their lives and their needs. Now write a succinct description of who your target market is.

Step 4: What will they love about your offer?

It is time to bring together Steps 1, 2 and 3.

Now you know:

- what you are selling
- the problems you are solving and how
- in detail, who you are selling to, and their needs.

It is time to think about what they will love most about your offer so you stand out from the crowd. Remember, most people buy things to:

- solve immediate problems
- make them more successful (for example, in money or relationships).

So ask yourself – what will they LOVE about your offering? I know it may seem strange to use the word LOVE – but when you can get your customers LOVING what you offer, that immediately gives you an advantage over the competition as you will have an emotional bond.

Think about what they will love. Here are some possible examples:

- your in-depth knowledge of the market
- trust in your expertise and experience
- the way you listen to their needs and find the perfect solution
- the look and feel of your brand
- it's made in the UK
- you offer caring customer support
- your product is easy to use and accessible
- it's a new product (i.e. they will be the first to use a new gadget).

What are the emotional benefits of them buying your product, and which will keep them coming back for more?

Step 5: Who is the competition and why are they different?

Even if you have a great product, chances are very high that there will be competition. In Chapter 6 you spent a lot of time analysing who else is in your space, and how you differ from them. Now summarise how you stand out from the competition.

Creating the value proposition has coalesced your work so far into one page. You have a succinct and specific description of what you are selling, to whom and why they will buy it.

You now have clarity about your idea.

Be savvy

In the introduction to this part I said you would be able to complete the value proposition Worksheet once you had worked through the chapters. Go back and print off the value proposition Worksheet now (www.CorporateCrossovers.com/MyNewBusiness). Write on it, scribble over it. Make it a living and breathing document while you are in this planning stage. Then use it in your briefings to designers, suppliers and partners. This will give them an insight into your business idea, and ensure that they are all working to the same brief. Enrolling partners in this way makes them feel more committed and engaged.

Busy woman's shortcut

Print out a copy of the value proposition Worksheet and keep it with you. Use it to capture random thoughts, ideas and observations as you go through your day. These can be added to the master copy and refined later.

Caution

This does not have to be perfect. If you find yourself getting caught up in the perfect phrasing or exact details, stop! Since this will evolve over time, as you acquire more information, start with what you have. Revisit and go back to it. Remember progress, not perfection!

Part

3

How do I plan for success?

A simple overview of a new business involves the following stages:

1. Come up with business idea

2. Make it

3. Work out how to sell it

4. Launch!

5. Promote it

6. You sell your offering for more than it cost you to make

7. Customers buy it and give you money

8. You keep some profit, and put some back into the business

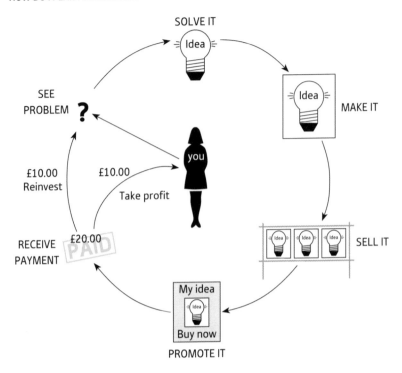

This is a very simplistic view of how a business works. To simplify it further, business is selling things for a higher price than it costs you to make them, and finding someone to buy at that price and thus making a profit.

If you take this simple view of business then there are three things that will underpin your success:

1. how much it costs to make your product
2. finding customers to buy it
3. pricing your offering so that you make a profit and so that it's an attractive price for the customer to buy once, and then continue to buy.

Now you are feeling more confident about your idea, it's time to consider how to start your business. How do you bring your idea to life and create a real business?

Chapter

How do I make it/do it?

It's time to roll up your sleeves and investigate how you will bring your wonderful idea to life. In this chapter you will discover:

- how to make your service or product
- how much it will cost to produce.

Now you have created your value proposition, and used your market research to refine it further, you will be feeling more confident that your idea will succeed. It's time to discover how to produce it at the cost your customer can afford.

There are two stages to this:

1. determining what the product or service will be made from and how it will be produced
2. estimating the cost of production.

Step 1: How will it be made?

Depending on your idea and your industry, you will have a different range of raw materials, ingredients, components or licences you need to buy to create your product.

You need to develop the list of ingredients or components to produce your offering. If you are stuck, a great place to start is to review your competitors. Can you discover what they use to make their products? This may be listed on their packaging, or it could be on their website or in industry journals. Visit trade shows to explore more about the industry sector and possible suppliers and producers.

Here are some examples of different sectors and their possible ingredients to get you started:

Retailer

- the products for sale in the shop, gift wrap, bags, food, condiments, cutlery, etc.

Manufacturer

- the raw materials to make your products, e.g. for cakes this might be flour, yeast, sugar, butter, etc.
- any packaging
- labour involved, e.g. in making the cake.

Knowledge-based business

- you are selling your time for money, so how much does your time cost?
- you may have workshop materials, licence fees, the use of other consultants, etc.

Services

- the cost of the products to provide the service, e.g. cleaning products and equipment if you are a cleaner, dog food if you are a dog walker, etc.

So, for example, a jewellery designer would need to think about the following:

- the chain, gems, clasps, rings, and other components to make each piece of jewellery
- the packaging for each piece
- the labour required to make it.

Once Hayley Gait-Golding, from BEAR, had made her first smoothie in her kitchen, baked it and realised she was on to something delicious, she knew she needed to find help to make it in large enough quantities: *'After identifying that the product was feasible and people liked the idea, I knew that I had to find a production partner. I had to find a fruit farmer first, so I went on the internet and found agricultural lists of farmers and growers around the world.'* Hayley called many of them and faced countless rejections. She persevered until, *'I found one guy who was really open minded and also shared the passion for health that I had.'*

She then went on to spend three weeks in his farm kitchen where they worked together: *'We tried recipe after recipe. It took about three weeks until we got our first recipe that we were happy with. That was the recipe we took to Waitrose, and they liked it. We got the listing and then we have just grown and evolved.'*

Step 2: How much will it cost?

Before you start to make decisions about precisely what ingredients or components you will use, it is most important that you know the approximate price that your customer will pay.

There is no point in making a product from the highest quality 'Harrods' ingredients when they only want to pay 'Iceland' prices. If you take this approach you risk losing money on every item you sell. And that's not a business proposition, that's an expensive hobby.

It may be that how you start with your suppliers is not ultimately where you end up. Tiffany London, founder of Tiffany Rose special occasion maternity wear, started her business using dresses from other dress designers: *'I started by buying in other people's designs and then selling in the UK.'* This was a low-risk way for her to understand more about the market place and how viable her business would be. As she says: *'I learnt much more about what customers wanted in terms of the price points they were prepared to pay, the quality of the fabric and how important the fit was to them.'* When she realised that her suppliers were no longer providing the quality she expected, she decided to take the plunge and create her own line of dresses and start her own label.

Calculating how much your service or product will cost to produce is essential to do at this planning phase. You need to know if your idea is financially viable at these initial stages so, if required, it is easy to make changes to your proposition.

The cost of goods, or cost of sales as they are also called, are all the costs that are incurred when you make your product, or get your service ready to sell.

The best way to estimate how much it will cost to make a product is to complete these three steps:

1. **What do you need?** Write a list of all the products, ingredients, raw materials, licences etc. that you will need to make your offering.

2. **For each item find three different suppliers.** Through your research into the market place, and your review of your competitors, you will probably have a good understanding of who are the suppliers.

3. **Contact suppliers.** Ask how much it will cost to buy what you require from them. You may also need to ask them the price for different quantities, so you can ensure that you understand what discount you will get for increased quantities.

 In order to work through the following Worksheets, you are going to need some advance information. Try to gather together as much of the following as possible before going on to work through the exercises:

- a list of all the supplies you need
- an estimate of how many xxx will you be ordering
- an idea of how often you may wish to order
- a list of possible suppliers and contact details (keep in mind your end user – is it the right quality for them?)
- contact them for price lists, terms of business, forms to complete if you are to become a customer
- lead times – how long will they take to supply you?
- references.

The beauty of doing this research now is that should one supplier be no longer able to supply you, then you have at your fingertips two other supply options. This will help reduce the risk to your business.

 ## Find your suppliers

To estimate the cost of making your product or service (cost of goods) you need to find your suppliers and obtain estimates for their supplies. To assist in determining the best supplier and the time required to bring your product to market, complete this form to investigate all options. Download the form (www. CorporateCrossovers.com/MyNewBusiness) and print off as many as you need.

Supplies needed	Quantity required	Frequency of order	Possible suppliers	Lead times/ seasonality considerations	Pricing

Once you have done this review, and before you select who you are going to use, I recommend that you research your suppliers thoroughly. This is because they will become absolutely critical to your business when you are operating. You need a supplier you can trust and rely upon.

Before you select your supplier, the bare minimum information you need is:

- how reliable they are
- what their payment terms are (for your cash flow)
- how quickly they deliver
- what their reputation is like
- how often they raise their prices.

If you believe a supplier will be a make or break point in your business, then ask them for references from other customers. Take the time to ring their customers and ask them how well that supplier meets their needs.

When you are thinking about creating and then selling your product for the first time, you must be cognisant of the lead times of supplying ingredients or components in order to calculate how long it will take you to get to market.

So, as part of your supplier research, you must ask about lead times (i.e. what is the length of time between you ordering your supplies and receiving them?) Also ask if this changes at seasonal times, for example whether they close for religious festivals or summer holidays. You need to know this to build it into your planning.

Tracy Mort of Grace Cole had traditionally sourced her gift boxes from China. Her business was skewed to sell these over the pre-Christmas period, meaning her sales were very strong August through December, and weak the rest of the year.

Contemplating how to boost her sales in the slow months, and facing the economic gloom in 2008 of more British companies going under, Tracy decided to produce a new line of daily care products made in the UK. 'I had never purchased from the UK. I'm very experienced buying from China, so it was like learning my craft all over again. I had to find new suppliers, find out if they were good, look at all the pricing, the quality of the packaging, the quality of the fill.'

Not only did she smooth her sales seasonality, she found a profitable need in the market: 'It was quite obvious that made in the UK products were in high demand and with the added value and the premium *positioning, I charged more for them. They have worked very well for us, significantly lifting our sales and margin.'*

Creating a 'Cost of Goods Sold' for your product

Now you have done the research into your potential suppliers and received price lists or quotes from them, it is time to make up an estimate of how much it will cost you to create the product.

Let's work through a simple example of a cake.

1. You buy your flour in bulk, at £20 per 50-kilo bag, and you only need one kilo for your cake.

2. Then you need to calculate how much a kilo of that flour has cost you … so if it is £20 for 50 kilos it will be £0.4 per kilo. This is the amount you need to add into your cake cost.

Likewise with labour. You must calculate how much time it will cost you to produce the item. Again, using the cake as an example, if you cost your time out at £10 per hour and you take 15 minutes to make the cake then, obviously it is £2.50 labour cost.

Raw materials	Bulk price	Cost of ingredients	Requirement for one cake	Cost
Flour	£20 for 50 kilos	£0.4/kilo	1 kilo	0.40
Sugar	£90 for 100 kilos	£0.9/kilo	500 grams	0.45
Butter	£30 for 10 kilos	£3/kilo	500 grams	1.50
Eggs	£8 for 100 eggs	£0.08/egg	2 eggs	0.16
Flavouring	£10 per kilo	£10/kilo	200gms	2.00
Packaging	£25 for 50 boxes	£0.50 each	1	0.50
Labour	£10 an hour		15 minutes	2.50
Licence fees (if any)	n/a			
Total Cost				£7.61

At this stage it is important to consider everything in your costing so you can get an accurate estimate of your financial exposure.

 ## Calculating cost of goods sold

Now calculate the cost of goods sold by completing the following chart (remember you can download it from **www.CorporateCrossovers.com/MyNewBusiness** and tailor it to your needs).

Product			
Raw material	Amount required	Cost per unit	Cost for product/ service
e.g. flour	500gm	£2/kilo	£0.50
Total cost of raw materials (A)			
Packaging			
Total cost of packaging (B)			
Licence fees (C)			
Delivery costs (D)			
Labour costs (E)			
Other costs			
Total other costs (F)			
Total cost of goods (A+B+C+D+E+F)			

Outsourcing to a third party

It may be that the product you wish to make is difficult to produce yourself, so you decide to outsource the production. Perhaps you want to manufacture fashion tights, and you do not want to invest in the equipment to make them. If this is the case, then you will need to find a manufacturer that you trust, is reliable and will create the product to your specifications, every time.

Clearly this is a very big decision and one that will require you to undertake 'due diligence', researching who could make it, selecting a shortlist and then rigorously ensuring that they are right for you. (In business terms 'due diligence' is an investigation or audit of a business, person or potential investment prior to signing a contract.)

When you are undertaking your due diligence consider these questions:

- What volume are you looking for?
- What is the company's track record in reliability and quality?
- Can you get references from existing customers?
- What would their service level agreement be (i.e. turnaround from order to delivery to you)?
- What is their quality assurance system?
- Do they have the capability, the skills, the machines, the people to be able to produce what you need?
- What is the guarantee?
- Do they have a returns policy?
- What are their payment terms?
- Where are they based – how convenient is this to you?

 Outsourcing

If you decide to outsource your production, create a shortlist of potential suppliers and ask questions such as these to begin your due diligence. Obviously, there will be other questions pertinent to your situation you will need to ask as well.

Jane Mitchell from Jane Plan had to use her investigative skills to find suppliers for her range of meals: '*If you're not already in the industry it is really hard because manufacturers do not promote themselves well. Attending trade shows was really important because no matter how much research I did on the internet, it never was quite the same as getting out there. The other way I found suppliers was going to places like Wholefoods and looking at the manufacturers on the shelves. I bought a lot of other people's foods and then read their packets because legally you have to say where it's cooked. Then I would google it and find they had got a little factory in Leeds.*'

There are a number of websites that will help you find supplies, and manufacturers:

- Alibaba (http://www.alibaba.com/)
- Manufacturing Advisory Service (http://www.mymas.org/)
- Department of Business, Innovation and Skills (https://www.gov.uk/government/organisations/department-for-business-innovation-skills)

Also look for industry trade journals and trade shows relevant to your own business.

Busy woman's shortcut

Start a spreadsheet or database now. It will help you keep track of all your investigations and save you time later.

Be savvy

I recommend you find three suppliers for everything in your business, and then you have a range of offerings from which to compare estimates and quotes for their work. This is best practice in business as it ensures that you get the best price and value. It will also increase your industry knowledge by encouraging you to seek out more suppliers in your domain.

Caution

When you are investigating outsourcing options, ask what their disaster recovery plan is. What happens if their equipment breaks, they are flooded or something else unexpected happens? How long will it take them to get up and running again, and what will you do in the meantime?

Chapter **10**

How will I sell it?

You are moving through the elements to bring your idea to life. Now you need to identify how you will get your offering to the end user. Will you sell it yourself, or will it be through other channels?

Working through this chapter will enable you to identify:

- where you could sell your offering
- what that may cost you.

How will your product or service physically reach your end user? Which sales channel will work best for you? Where you sell your offering needs to be carefully considered, not only in terms of the ease of which your customer can find your offering but also in how well you be represented by that particular sales channel. Do they match your brand? Will you be well represented there?

Think again about your ideal customer. Refer back to the work you did in Chapter 7. Where are they most likely to buy your offering?

It could be from one or more of these sales channels:

- your own shop
- someone else's physical shop (e.g. a supermarket, restaurant, gift store, etc.)
- your own website
- directly from you in person (e.g. a consultant, coach, therapist)
- a distributor or wholesaler
- an agency (for them to use with their client)
- another website (e.g. Etsy, eBay, Not On The High Street)
- home-selling parties
- at fairs, school fêtes, trade shows, etc.

Go back to your initial work about your target market and consider how they would buy this product or service from you. Review what your competition is doing as well. It may be that you have more than one way that your customers can buy from you.

A past client of mine created the most beautiful sterling silver jewellery inspired by her home in Zimbabwe. She sold direct from her website and at fairs, and also through specially selected shops who matched her brand image. The dual approach worked well for her, as she still had the direct contact with the women who would be wearing her pieces, and the shops gave her access to more customers.

If you are a service-based industry, for instance a coach, it may be that you have clients who come directly to you, and you also work as an associate for a bigger coaching firm. This can be a great way to get established, and to build your confidence when you are first starting out.

> Montezuma's had a dream of being a high-end retail chain across the UK. Starting up, it never really considered selling to other retailers.
>
> As Helen recalls: *'At the start, we had people coming into the Brighton shop and say "Oh, I've got a deli in Hove. Can I sell your stuff?" Initially we had to say no, because we couldn't make it quick enough. But then we moved into a bigger place with more production capacity. Once we'd moved and made that leap into the next size of production unit, then we had capacity. We went back to talk to these people and said, "Well actually, yes we can supply your deli". And that all happened, almost by accident. So we started supplying into other retailers unintentionally. But now, the biggest part of the business is selling into other retailers.'*

 ## Identify distribution channels

A distribution channel is how you will distribute your product or service to your customer. Revisit your initial work about your target market and consider how they would buy this product or service from you. Consider what your competition is doing as well. It may be that you have more than one distribution channel – or more than one way that your customers can buy from you.

List the most suitable ways your prospect could buy.

Distribution partners

If you have identified that the best way for you to reach your ideal customer is through a third party, then you need to do the same level of research with these distribution partners as you did with your suppliers. These organisations will be key to your success, as they may be the only way you reach your customer. The more you know about what they require, the better your chance of success will be.

Think of these organisations as your business partners. That is, if they do well and sell lots of your offering, then you will do well. They make more profit, and so do you.

Having this shared approach to success and treating your distributors as partners will enhance your relationship. You will believe that you are on the same side, sharing the intention of selling more. You both win!

I know from my own experience and that of my clients that this approach will affect the tone of your meetings and emails and enable you to create compelling promotional ideas that will sell more of your product and help you both.

A client of mine created beautiful handmade purses. She was frustrated that sales of her bags had declined in a funky gift shop that previously had been selling very well. What she discovered in her next phone call with them, was that a new manager had taken over and was rearranging the displays, and my client's products had been pushed to the bottom shelf. Her beautiful purses were no longer easily visible to a passing shopper.

After our coaching call, my client decided to meet with the new manager to try to improve her sales. My client and I had calculated how much extra profit the shop would make if it displayed the purses more visibly and in a bigger display case. She went to the meeting with photos of her purses in other shops and discussed with the manager the impact of the larger displays on sales and profit. The manager saw the money she was missing and so reinstalled my client's products to the main display cabinet again.

Your ideal distribution partner will depend on your business. If you have a service which is relevant for professional services firms to sell to their clients, then they would be an ideal distribution partner, for instance if you made accounting software, an obvious distribution partner would be accounting firms.

Blippar is a new app that enables users to scan products and unleash special interactive content on their device. It is coveted by advertisers and ad agencies to make their products and campaigns more compelling.

Blippar is now used extensively by well-known brands, for example, Heinz, Coca-Cola, L'Oréal, Jaguar and Virgin. The key to getting to these brands and their advertising budgets is through advertising agencies. They are a key distribution channel for Blippar.

As Jess Butcher explains: '*I spend a lot of time educating and evangelising Blippar to agencies and brands to constantly get the best practice ideas out there, to do case studies.*'

Selling via large retailers

If you need to sell through large retailers, you must fully research all of their requirements to take on new products. These may be costly and time-consuming for small suppliers. A large retailer will want to ensure the following before giving you an order:

- Can your business cope with large orders?
- Are you legal (e.g. covered by food and hygiene regulations, or safety regulations)?
- Are you EU compliant in your area?
- Is your labelling correct (especially regarding food ingredients)?

They may also undertake other due diligence such as your financial viability and your plans to market your product and build your brand.

Again, it's important to treat them as your partner. Ask them what they require for this product to be a success. Get their opinion on your packaging, your branding and your promotional ideas. The more involved they feel, the more they will support you.

When dealing with large retailers there may also be additional fees that you need to pay to be accepted into their stores. They may include the following:

- listing fees
- slotting fees
- after-sale rebates
- promotional fees
- co-operative advertising.

Research and speaking with other businesses that supply your target retailer can assist you in discovering these charges and being able to plan for them. You will also be able to gain information on how best to work with these retailers.

Selling on the web

If you are planning to sell direct via a website, then in addition to your own site, you may want to research what other sites could promote and sell your offering. This is similar to selling direct to your own customers and then selling in someone else's shop as well. It is an efficient way of getting your offering in front of many more prospects. Utilise the work that other businesses have done in growing their traffic and customer lists.

Joint-venture arrangements are very common in the online market, and you may find many people willing to promote your product or service for a fee. If you consider this, remember the site you will be listed on will be seen as an extension of your brand, so ensure that it is a brand you are proud to be associated with.

Catherine Watkin, creator of Selling from the Heart, uses distribution partners for her sales training and mentoring business: *'I started to do joint ventures which initially I found really hard. I questioned if I could ever ask anybody to help me. I summoned up the courage to ask, and in January I launched my online programme again. But this time I did it with joint venture partners and instead of 20 sign ups I had 81.'*

Distribution channel research

Once you have selected your ideal distribution channel, then you need to understand what they require from you, and what fees may be involved. For you to calculate your pricing model, you also need to know what profit they want to make from selling your goods or services.

Ask these questions:

- What do they require from their suppliers?
- How long does it take for them to make a decision?
- How many people are involved in the decision-making process?
- Do they charge listing fees?

- What are their mark-ups?

- What are their promotional charges?

- What do they need to see to make their decision – website, prototype, a real sample, customer testimonials, lab reports, research results?

Getting into your identified distribution channel – tenacity!

Once you have identified your ideal distribution channels, consider if you have a contact there, or if you know the name of the key buyer. For example, if you are selling via school fairs, this might be the name of the head of the PTA. Or if you are selling into HR departments, the name of the HR director.

Then start your research, and again, this will be an iterative process… you will keep adding to this information as you do your research and discover new data.

From the experience of my clients I know it takes many months and phone calls to get an appointment with a buyer at a large retailer. Passion and tenacity are key!

Getting into the supermarkets was a big win for Hayley of BEAR but, as she says, it wasn't easy: *'Its about not quitting and keeping going no matter how many times you get told no. You get used to a healthy dose of rejection and one day your persistence pays off.'*

Caution

Before you approach the big retailers, know what your plan is to produce large volumes. They will ask how you can meet their volume demands. The more prepared you are for this question, the more confidently you can approach the meeting.

Busy woman's shortcut

When you do your competitor research, keep a note of how they reach their customer. This could become your potential distribution plan too.

Be savvy

Remember you only have one chance to make a first impression. How can you 'wow' the potential distribution partner the first time you meet them? They need to feel impressed and confident that you will deliver your offering on time and at the specification ordered. They also need to know that you will come up with ideas that help them to sell more of your offering.

Chapter

What shall I charge for it?

Setting the right pricing models are imperative to ensure that your business is a success. You want to make money from all of your hard work and great ideas. In this chapter, discover:

- what to charge for your offering
- how much profit you will make.

Setting the right prices and then feeling confident about your pricing model can be one of the more challenging aspects of setting up a business. If you charge too little, you don't make enough profit and people may not value you or your offering. Charge too much and you may feel that you are putting people off by being too expensive, or you may think you are not worthy of receiving that much.

Developing your pricing model is a combination of science, art and confidence:

- science, because you know how much the item costs to create and how much you need to charge to make a profit
- an art, because you need to imagine what your customer will pay
- confidence, because you have to believe that you are worth charging that amount and have the chutzpah to ask for it.

When you are producing a product, I think it is easier to determine what you can charge. Your competitive analysis will have given you valuable information about the range of prices in the market, and also the quality of ingredients used in the product. You can assess where you sit in the market, and the appropriate price point to represent that.

In a service business, setting the price can be a little more difficult. How do you know how much you are worth compared to the next coach, massage therapist, accountant or lawyer?

The easiest place to start is with the science. Develop a pricing chart of the market and your closest competitors.

Then think about all of the elements that make up your offering:

- your years of experience
- your training
- your credentials
- your current client list
- your unique approach, etc.

Lastly, how much do you feel comfortable asking for? When you need to look a prospect in the eye, what is that number you will firmly believe that you are worth?

Developing pricing models

So far, you have done a lot of work in gathering the data you need to make sound decisions about pricing. You have a good understanding of:

- how you will make your offering
- who will provide the supplies you need

- how you will get your product to market
- what additional costs may be involved.

It is now time to bring together your investigations from the previous chapters. Gather together the following:

- the costs to produce your product or service
- information about how you will sell it, and if any costs will be involved
- the research on your competitors' pricing
- feedback from your prospects about pricing
- information about the market, and where your idea will fit.

Creating an effective pricing model will be an iterative process. You may select one price, then once you have put it through your costing model, realise you make no profit on it. Back to the drawing board in that case!

Step 1: Determine your selling price based on the market

Use the Worksheets below to assist you with creating a range of price points to put into your model.

 ### Possible price points

Gather together the information from your research of the market and your competitive analysis and list your competitors' price points.

Competitors' pricing	A	B	C	D	E	F

Consider how you want to be positioned in the market. Do you want to be affordable and great value for money, like Tesco, or would you prefer to be exclusive and high end, like Harrods? Thinking about where you want your product to be positioned will also help you determine your pricing level.

Possible prices	Low	Medium	High

Determine a range of price points that you want to test out. These numbers will go into your spreadsheet to determine how profitable each price point is.

Price point options	A	B	C	D

When Tracy Mort designed her range of gift boxes for the Christmas market, she knew the type of person she wanted to buy them, and therefore her positioning came from that: '*I wanted to target the shopper who really thought about the person they were buying it for. They would buy them a beautiful, luxury gift of high quality because they treasured that person. I knew what I had to buy it for from my suppliers and I then knew what I had to sell it for to make sure the profit margins were correct. The price was set at the level to represent the quality of the product.*'

Step 2: Will you make profit at that pricing?

Now you have a range of possible prices, you need to understand if you will make any money, and if so, how much. This adds more information to the mix to help you to determine what the right price is.

Create a spreadsheet to make this as easy as possible. You want to be able to analyse a range of possible price points so you can understand how much profit you will make from each pricing option.

Use the information below to create your own spreadsheet on Excel, or simply complete this by hand.

You need the following data:

- cost of goods information
- distribution channel fees.

The purpose of this work is to calculate your profit per unit. This will then provide a foundation as you build the rest of the financial models for the business. It may take you a few attempts to get the calculations at the price you feel most confident charging and to make the profit you desire.

This is an iterative process, and believe it or not, you may find it fun to play around with the numbers to see how high or low you could go.

The beauty of doing this detailed work on pricing now, is that when someone does ask you, 'How much do you charge?' you will know that you have done the work and have the foundations in place to be able to answer that question with confidence.

Web design expert Keren Lerner discusses how she approaches her pricing strategy and the impact it has on business: '*I realised I needed to change my pricing because of the time we spend on projects and the work we do – I didn't want to reduce the quality of the work we did or the value we bring, so it meant we needed to increase prices. I was on a plane and I wrote down a whole bunch of numbers and I then just wrote double numbers for our project pricing, based on the effort and time spent. It was necessary to manage costs without losing on the quality.*'

Because staff at Keren's company track the time they spend on client's projects through time sheets, she was able to easily see exactly what her costs were in relation to each project. She had the data to make an informed decision confidently.

VAT

Do you need to consider VAT? It depends.

1. If you are selling a VAT applicable product or service and your turnover is more than £79,000 you will need to add VAT to each item you sell.

2. If you are selling through a large retailer, they will add the 20 per cent VAT to the retail price. This will increase your price to the end user, whether or not you charge VAT to the retailer.

The HMRC website has considerable information on this. If in doubt, phone them (details can be found on their website: www. hmrc.gov.uk).

When determining the pricing of her first dresses, Tiffany London of Tiffany Rose special occasion maternity wear, describes how she did it: *'When I decided to launch my own label I had to work out whether or not it would be viable. I did it in an Excel spreadsheet, and developed the numbers very simply. I could understand it clearly, and saw what I had to do. I saw what price range I'd be looking at having to sell the clothes at, based on the costs that I would incur.'*

 Pricing models

Complete the following chart to get started on your own pricing. An example has been given here to help, but you can download the worksheet (**www.CorporateCrossovers.com/ MyNewBusiness**) to complete it for your own business.

	Jewellery example
Recommended Retail Price per unit (what you think your prospect will pay)	£23.40 plus VAT (234% mark-up on wholesale)
Distributor profit (also called margin; sometimes you will be given a percentage mark-up on your wholesale price for the retail price – in the example 234%; the distributor profit is the difference between your wholesale price and their retail price)	£13.40

Wholesale price per unit (the price you will sell your product/service to the distribution channel)	£10
Cost of goods per unit (the amount you have calculated it will cost you to create the product or service per unit)	£2.50
Gross profit per unit (the wholesale price less the cost of goods)	£7.50

If you are selling your product or service direct, then your pricing model will be as follows:

	Jewellery example
Recommended Retail Price per unit (what you think your prospect will pay)	£23.40 plus VAT
Cost of goods per unit (the amount you have calculated it will cost you to create the product or service per unit)	£2.50
Gross profit per unit (the retail price less the cost of goods)	£20.90

It may take you several attempts to get the numbers working in a way that feels right. As mentioned above, it is the balance between having the right price for your market, and also making enough profit per unit.

This is the profit you are making for each unit sold, and this is called Gross Profit. Some of that profit still has to go into running the business. You will use this money to pay for rent, stationery, utilities etc. Once they have been taken away, then you will have Net Profit left over, and this is the true figure of how much your business will make. We will cover this in Chapter 14.

Step 3: Being confident about what you charge

The other factor with pricing is the confidence you demonstrate when you are asking for the price. Based on my own experience and that of my clients we typically undercall our prices. And this is much more to do with what we think we are worth than what we think our customers will pay.

Too often clients of mine describe how they hesitate, look down and gently mention their asking price. Inside they are squirming! And thinking, 'Oh maybe I should have made it less, maybe it's too much and they'll say no.'

Before you start getting into situations where you will have to share your prices, be prepared. Get confident about your pricing strategy by truly understanding and owning your value.

 ## Three steps to state your price with confidence

1. **Market research.** Is your price set at the right level? Check out the competition and make a note of what your prospects will pay.

2. **You deserve it.** Write a list of 20 (yes 20) reasons why you deserve to be paid that much (experience, training, clients, etc.). This will bolster your self-belief in why you are worth this much.

3. **Know your value.** It is imperative that you know and totally believe in the value that your offering gives your customers. When you believe, they will as well. Write a list of the 20 ways in which customers benefit from working with you.

Be savvy

If you feel uncomfortable talking about prices, fees or rates then do try the following:

1. Create a pricing page that looks professional – call this your rate card.

2. Practise asking for that amount of money before asking for it with a real customer.

Busy woman's shortcut

Plan your price rises six months in advance. This will allow you enough time to inform current customers, update your website and rate card. And it will give you time to become fully confident about communicating the higher price.

Caution

Keep an eye on the market at all times. I was an executive coach in London in 2008 when the financial crisis happened. Many of my clients slashed their Learning and Development budgets. I knew I had to keep my price the same and add more value to keep the business. If price is an issue, then think about what other value you can add to sweeten the deal.

12

How do I market it?

Creating a plan to bring new customers to your business will increase your confidence about how successful you will be. New customers are the lifeblood of every business and without them you will fail.

In this chapter you will discover:

- how to reach your target
- what your compelling marketing message needs to be to attract
- the steps to create your marketing plan.

'Build a better mousetrap, and the world will beat a path to your door' is a phrase attributed to Ralph Waldo Emerson. I'm sure you have heard this before. And by and large it's true, but only if the world knows about it and cares enough to stop what they are doing right now, to start the journey to your door.

No matter how amazing the new mousetrap is, it will always be a business failure if no one knows about it. That's why marketing plays a critical part in your business success.

Before someone can buy your unique, well-priced offering, they need to know about it. And once they know it exists, they have to like it. Then, before they move to purchase, they have to trust that it will solve their problems in a way that is worth the money.

Marketing is all about moving someone through a journey with you. An excursion starting with zero awareness, and ending at purchase. They need to walk the Know, Like, Trust path with you before they will buy.

Know — Your prospect sees you and develops an awareness of you and what you offer.

Like — Your prospect may 'meet' you again, see your ad or social media post, increase their understanding of you and your offer and form a positive opinion about it.

Trust — Through repeated 'meetings', your prospect interacts with you and your offer more and their opinion of you deepens. They may start to seek you out, mention you to others and start to think about how you would fit in their lives. They see how you deliver what you say you do.

Buy — The prospect buys! They believe that your offer will solve their pain and it is worth an exchange of their money for your service.

Think about how you form friendships. It is very unlikely that you go from meeting a stranger to, in that same meeting, sharing your most intimate secrets with them and inviting them to a small family gathering. Building friendships takes time. At each meeting you share a little more about yourselves and the trust builds. Then over time, you have a very close and meaningful relationship.

I like to think of marketing in business as the same. That on the first viewing of you, your blog or product on the shelf, they may not buy, but they will become interested. And then over time, with repeated exposure and you doing what you say you would do, to build credibility, this all forms a stronger, trusting relationship.

Years ago, I worked as marketing manager for Colgate toothpaste. We knew that when we launched a new toothpaste variant, like Tartar Control, that the audience who saw the ad wouldn't rush out and buy it after seeing it for the first time on TV. They had to see that advertisement at least seven times before their interest and desire was piqued enough to purchase it when they went to the supermarket. After seeing the ad seven times, they knew Colgate Tartar Control existed (KNOW), they started to LIKE us because the ad spoke to their oral care problems, and they TRUSTED us, because of the brand Colgate and they had seen the ad so often.

Marketing your business is no different. The medium you use to reach your prospects and the message you use will differ, but the concepts of Know, Like and Trust hold true.

Here are some examples of different activities that fall into the Know, Like, Trust marketing model.

Know, Like, Trust examples

Know	• Networking
	• Advertising – radio, TV, magazines, newspapers, other peoples' websites, billboards
	• Websites
	• Articles in magazines, newspapers
	• Sponsorship
	• Blogging
	• Facebook posts
	• Google
	• LinkedIn networking
	• Tweeting
	• Instagram
	• Pinterest
	• Postcards
	• Flyers
	• Sign writing on vehicles
	• Shop windows
Like	• Repeated exposure of the above
	• Networking follow up, meeting for coffee
	• Speaking to groups
	• Follow/like on social media, engage in conversations
	• Read blog, articles
	• Visit website and sign up for newsletter
	• Come into shop
	• Ring, email enquiries
	• Free trial
Trust	• Repeated exposure of the above
	• Repeat networking and one-on-one meetings
	• Word of mouth
	• Referrals
	• Testimonials
	• Join free interactions (newsletter, free calls, events)

So, what will work for me?

It is easy to get overwhelmed by the concept of marketing and all the activity that can come with it – especially in these days of social media. You may be thinking you need to tweet, blog, pin, advertise in local press, hire a public relations person.

Before you do anything, always go back to WHO you want to buy your offering, and HOW they receive new information about solutions to their problems.

In marketing, I believe less is more. That is, you are better to choose one or two places to start, and be consistent in your activity. Consistency is critical to build LIKE and TRUST. People need to see that you are a trusted company; stable and repeated exposure in the same medium will do this. Flitting from one social media channel to the next won't.

Focusing on just two marketing strategies worked well for Catherine Watkin of Selling from the Heart: '*I played to my strengths last year. I focused on two main marketing strategies and I stuck to them.*' She chose public speaking and joint ventures to grow her awareness (Know and Like). By leveraging her partners' audiences she was able to double the interest in her courses and grow her revenues.

The other important piece to consider with your marketing is what do you like to do? If public speaking fills you with dread, then giving talks to networking groups will not be a successful marketing approach. Yet, if you love writing, then offering to guest blog, or write pieces in magazines to raise your profile could be perfect. This is especially important to think about if you are launching on a budget and you will be the marketing department.

Alicia Cowan also talks of the impact she has had from being disciplined in her marketing approach: '*My early success was really down to me focusing on one social media platform. I chose Twitter and blogging, and that was all that I did. I recognise the benefit of not spreading yourself too thinly and really focusing your energies on the right tasks and the right areas of the business, particularly when it comes to marketing.*'

She goes on to say: '*Embrace the internet and what it can do for your business and because it is the coolest, most powerful marketing tool that we have in the modern world and in business, and we can really use it to create the business that we dream of and we want for ourselves.*'

Cutting through the noise

A study conducted by a leading consumer market research and analytics company[1] stated that between 3000 and 5000 advertisements are seen on a daily average. So how do you get noticed?

You need to be in the right place, with the right message at the right time.

By now, if you have been working through the exercises in this book, you will have a very good understanding of the following:

- your ideal customer and their make-up
- what their pains and problems are
- where they receive new information
- what you are offering to solve their problems.

An effective marketing plan takes into account all of these elements and weaves them together to create a pathway through the Know, Like and Trust buying journey.

To create your marketing plan, complete these six steps:

Step 1: Who is your prospect?

You must start with who you are trying to attract. You have already completed some great work back in Chapter 7. Revisit this to refresh your thinking.

Step 2: Where will you reach them?

Consider where they find out about new products and services. Is it from networking groups, the web, talks, articles, etc. Again, you have thought about this in previous chapters. Revisit the results of your market research and see if there are any clues in there.

Step 3: What do you say?

To break through the noise of all the other messages that customers are exposed to, you must focus in on their pains and how you will solve them. Go back to your value proposition you created in Part 2.

---

1 Yankelvich Research (**http://the futurescompany.com**)

You have already done some solid thinking about how your offering solves their problems, and, as important, what makes you different to the competition. Craft your marketing message by thinking about what you say to attract their attention, and entice them to read more.

Remember to always think about what you are saying from your customers' perspective. Will they care about what you are saying? Is it relevant? Does it speak to their pains? And most importantly, is it strong enough to break their inertia?

Step 4: What are your ideas?

Time to get creative! Brainstorm a list of ideas for your possible marketing activities.

Go back to the Know, Like and Trust examples, and create activities for each stage that will match with where your prospect likes to discover new information.

Your ideas will be a coalescence of:

- what you like to do
- where your message will be seen and responded to favourably
- how you take someone through the Know, Like, Trust journey.

If you are starting with a small amount of money, you will need to be inventive in how you raise awareness of your offering. Do you write a column for a magazine that you know your target market will read? Do you print off postcards and place them in the letter boxes of your desired suburb?

Again, always come back to what will reach your ideal customer. Anything else is wastage.

Step 5: What will it cost?

Research to see what costs are involved in your ideas. How much would an ad in the local parents' magazine cost, or an annual subscription to join a networking group? And remember to factor in the cost of your time.

Step 6: When will you implement your ideas?

When is the best time to do your marketing activity? If you are selling a great product for Christmas gifts, do you need to start marketing in November? Or if you sell weight loss products, do you start promoting in spring to help your clients get ready for swimsuit season?

You may have new products or design lines planned to coincide with the new seasons. Do you need to have an extra marketing push then as well? It's important to align your marketing activity with your business plans so that you can give any launches the best chance of success.

Think too about the activities of other businesses that may be aligned with what you are doing. Is there any way that you could dovetail your activity with them?

> At the bare minimum, no matter what level of marketing investment you choose, there are some basics you must do. Keren Lerner of Top Left Design explains: '*Get your house in order, even if you are only going to be going to networking events. Register a proper domain name, get an email address that matches the domain name and make a business card with the email address that matches the domain name. Put up a holding page with your branding and contact information. These are the first basic steps that show you are professional about what you do.*'

 Marketing plan

Work through the following questions to get started on your marketing plan (remember the Worksheet is downloadable from **www.CorporateCrossovers.com/MyNewBusiness** if you need more space).

Step 1: Who is your prospect?

Step 2: Where will you reach them?

Step 3: What do you say?

Step 4: What are your ideas?

Step 5: What will it cost?

Step 6: When will you implement your ideas?

From my experience of talking with hundreds of business owners over the years, many of them spend more time planning their summer holiday than creating a marketing plan to drive sales.

Creating a monthly or even weekly plan of marketing activity will give you:

- confidence that you are active in driving sales
- the ability to budget for marketing expenditure and thus manage your cash flow
- the knowledge that you have enough of the right marketing activity planned to drive sales when you are launching new lines, or new services.

Cleopatra from Celtic Quest Coasteering remembers how she started learning marketing: '*I just came up with an idea and worked out how can we do this, asked if anyone else had done it, and then worked out how much is it going to cost. I'd do my return on investment. Then if it looked like it would be worthwhile then we'd give it a crack. Sometimes it worked and sometimes it flopped.*'

Since then she has a more structured approach to her marketing: '*This is the second year where we have had a proper marketing strategy and a plan, actually in writing, not just all sorts of wild ideas. I have done the research from past years and now I have a better feel for what works.*'

Marketing plan and budget

Use this Worksheet to plot your first year's marketing plan and budget. Remember the Worksheet is downloadable (**www. CorporateCrossovers.com/MyNewBusiness**) so you have plenty of space to adapt it to your own business.

Year 1 marketing activity and budget

Month	1	2	3	4	5	6	7	8	9	10	11	12	Total cost
Activity estimated cost													
Activity estimated cost													
Activity estimated cost													
Activity estimated cost													
Activity estimated cost													
Activity estimated cost													
Total cost													

Caution

Social media may be free but in reality it comes at a cost: your time. Before you embark on a multi-faceted Facebook, Pinterest, Instagram, LinkedIn and Twitter extravaganza, think carefully about where your ideal prospect is most likely to be. Choose two channels and create a consistent, targeted presence.

Busy woman's shortcut

If the thought of creating a marketing plan from scratch fills you with dread, then find a Business Buddy and do it together. Imagine your target market and brainstorm the activities you could do. Two heads are better than one in this case, and this approach will save you time and be great fun!

Be savvy

Make time to review the impact of your marketing investments. It is easy to measure the impact it has had. How many sales have you had? Make time every month to review your marketing efforts against your targets, and if need be, adjust. Get in the habit of reviewing regularly.

Part

How will the business operate?

By now you will have the clarity about what your business idea is, and growing confidence about how you will attract customers and sell to them. Your offering is starting to take shape as you research how it will be made, where it will be sold and develop your pricing model.

Now we need to work on how the business will operate. Clarifying your offering, and what you will sell or do, is at the core of the business. Around that are the elements you need to consider to actually run your business. These elements are just as important to your long-term success as devising a compelling idea and marketing plan to support it.

Finances
- Invoicing
- Tax
- VAT
- Cash flow
- Profit and loss

Business Structure
- Infrastructure – telecommunications, internet, computer, utilities
- Human resources – people to support you
- Legal – company structures, governance, insurance, data protection
- Premises – where you will work

My core offering. What I do or sell

Business Knowledge
- Marketing
- Sales
- Customer relationships
- Financial acumen
- Leading people

Funding
- Time until first sale
- Cash flow
- How long until profit
- Sources of funding

The model above shows many of the elements needed to run a business. They include:

- What support do you require to make it happen?
- Do you require staff with specialist skills to handle the workload?
- Where are you going to work from?
- Do you require any specialist equipment or technology to start?
- How will you fund it?
- What legal structure is best for you?
- Have you thought about the finances, tax, bookkeeping, etc?

These types of questions need to be considered when you are planning how your business will operate. What do you need in place to get your offering to market?

You may decide to do most things yourself, and run the business from your laptop in the spare room. Many businesses start on the legendary kitchen table. This can be a great way to keep overheads down when you first begin. You may decide to grow organically as the business grows, covering all costs and investments with profit from the business.

However, if you are planning a bigger enterprise, then you may need to consider additional staff, premises, specialist equipment and invest in infrastructure.

In Part 4, we will cover the following:

- the best business structure to support you and your idea
- the financials – how much will you make?
- business knowledge – what must you know to succeed?
- funding options if your cash flow won't support you.

13

How will I make the business run?

Investigating business structure at this stage will help you avoid costly mistakes later on. Not only do you need to know how to be legal and protected, but you also need to consider how you are best supported to create a business that operates smoothly.

It's time to delve into the detail. In this chapter you will discover how to:

- estimate how many staff you need and how to find them, cheaply
- structure your business entity in the best way for you
- manage getting your money in and out of the business.

Developing the framework to support you and your business will be determined by how you want your business to be. Go back to your visioning and reasons why you wanted to start the business you completed in Part 1.

How your business will be structured and operate will be completely different if you want a small and flexible operation (to allow you to have more time with the children, for example) versus creating a large enterprise for your long-term financial freedom.

Another consideration with developing your business framework is your attitude towards risk and funding.

If you have an appetite for risk and are prepared to go out and seek funding, then you may start with large premises, new equipment and staff. On the other hand, if you prefer to reduce risk and self-fund your growth, then you will be taking a more organic approach to your business framework, only investing in offices, staff etc. when you have the cash flow to afford it. Either approach is as valid as the other, again it depends on your business, your aspirations and your temperament.

Many business owners start modestly, working from home, doing it all themselves. As their business starts to grow, they outsource certain aspects, take on a key staff member or move to larger premises. For many, this organic approach to their business framework has been very successful.

In developing your framework, you need to consider these key areas:

1. Human resources – people to support you
2. Premises – where you work
3. Legal – business structure, governance, insurance, data protection
4. Finances – invoicing, profit and loss, cash flow, VAT, tax, funding
5. Infrastructure – telecommunications, internet, utilities
6. Tracking and measurement of progress

1 Human resources – will you need staff?

Will you need people to help you make your business idea come to life and be a success? Or will you do it all yourself?

Take some time to think about your business and what areas you may need assistance in. It may be that you start doing it all yourself, but after a few months, you begin to acquire more resources. Planning this now will help you make decisions faster, so you can keep up with your business growth.

Acquiring resources for your business falls into two areas:

1. extra manpower to alleviate your work load (e.g. a virtual assistant to manage your diary and administration tasks, a social media manager to do your LinkedIn updates and tweeting)

2. specialist skills that you don't have and do not wish to learn (e.g. an accountant or web designer).

What staff do you need?

To develop the team you need to support you, go through this two-step process. When you create a business it can be tempting to do it all yourself because you think you are saving money. This is a misconception as you will end up doing many of the low value tasks yourself when you could be adding value elsewhere.

Step 1: What needs to be done?

Write down, or mind map, all of the different tasks that you need help with in your business. Think about what you need right now, and also think about what you will need in 12 months. Your business will be growing and so what you need now, will be less extensive than in 12 months' time. Plan now to capture these extra requirements so you can be sure to hire the right help.

Here's a few to get your thinking started:

Diary management	Selling to prospects
Taking orders	Sending packages
Updating Facebook	Invoicing
Developing partnerships	Tracking expenses
VAT returns	Developing new products
Networking	Booking in trade shows
Packing the product	Updating website
Dealing with suppliers	Getting samples
Chasing up invoices	Organising trade days

Depending on your business, you may have a completely different list.

Step 2: Group similar tasks

Then group all of the similar tasks together. It may be that when you start, you end up completing all of the tasks yourself, but as you grow and cash flow increases, you can begin to outsource (e.g. virtual assistant, social media manager, packaging and orders, customer relations etc). For instance, all of those tasks involved with money (e.g. invoicing, tracking expenses, VAT, tax, etc.) would sit well in the same group.

Once you have grouped all of the tasks, you will be able to see quite easily the roles that you need in your business.

Many business owners start by doing it all themselves. Tiffany London remembers: '*In the early days when I was doing everything myself, I was customer services, I was the packer, I was the buyer. I was everything. You don't get to take any holidays.*' Tiffany worked out her staff requirements by thinking about future success: '*We looked at where we wanted the business to be in three to five years. We wanted to work out what had to be happening for us to be successful. Then we worked backwards to work out who were the people that were going to help us get there and who we were going to have to have in place.*'

Tiffany also thought more about her needs: '*We also looked at lifestyle. I was stretched in all and every direction and so I wanted to find out where I would get the quickest relief.*' For Tiffany that was someone to take over the packing of the clothes and speaking with customers. She was delighted to say that that staff member is still a vital part of their business today. Ten years on she has 18 full-time staff with a dedicated warehouse and design studio.

Once you have got an idea of the work that needs to be done to support your business, then you need to decide who will do it. If it's not you, you also need to estimate how much it will cost you to get support, and where you will find that person.

Plan a staggered approach to attaining extra resources, so they grow at the same pace as your business. Ideally you want to avoid stuffing envelopes at midnight and sitting there wishing you had got in that additional help a few months ago. If you get to that point, you will be too busy to even look for help. Think about it now, and research what cost-effective and flexible options are out there that would suit you, before you need to make that midnight call.

The beauty of the internet and the trend for more people to work from home is that there is now a plethora of extremely experienced and able people who don't want traditional work any more, they are happy to work on a contract basis and be paid by the hour.

This is a fantastic resource for the small business owner, as you can then hire in help when you need it and when your cash flow is abundant enough to afford it.

Here is a list of resources I have used in the past to support my business at different stages. I recommend testing them out with a small piece of work, and then if you are happy and your trust is building, grow it from there.

Resources

Job bid sites

These are a fantastic resource for when you need a discrete piece of work done. If you are new to outsourcing then it is a great way to test the water with someone new on a non-risky task.

Job bid sites allow you to you post the piece of work you want completed, and people from all over the world bid on it outlining their experience and pricing.

I have used it for Search Engine Optimisation work on my website, specific coding I needed done that my normal web developer couldn't do, social media assistance and some logo work.

There is a vast array of talent and experience available so I recommend you take some time to view their offerings:

- www.elance.com
- www.peopleperhour.com
- www.odesk.com
- www.guru.com
- www.freelancer.com
- www.fiverr.com

Virtual assistance services

If you want someone to manage your diary, run errands, support you through a launch, project manage an event or create a system to manage your suppliers and customers, then consider hiring a virtual assistant. These are like a personal assistant, but are not located in your office.

You can find someone located in the UK, and I would recommend a Google search or ask. Word of mouth is the best way to find someone who will become a key part of your business. You need to trust them, and like their approach as they may speak with your clients, prospects and business partners.

When you are interviewing your VA, you would treat it like a normal job interview. Before the interview compose a job description. You could include:

- a list of the tasks you would like them to be responsible for
- what decisions they will make
- who they will be interacting with
- what budget sign-off they have (if any)
- how many hours you need them
- which days you would like them to work
- where you would like them to work.

From this brief job description you can compose a list of questions that will enable you to ascertain if they have the right skills and experience you need. Be certain to ask for references from past or current clients and phone them to follow up.

There are also large virtual assistance organisations offshore, who will assign you an account manager and work with you to do the work you need. I used one of these for five years and they were great for typing, creating PowerPoint presentations and completing research.

These offer pay by the hour payment arrangements and you can use your credit card.

- www.fancyhands.com
- www.brickworkindia.com
- www.getfriday.com

Ad hoc staff

You may require staff at certain times of the year, especially if you are a retailer, or have some large launch events planned. In these cases, ad-hoc staff would be a great solution for your support. These are staff that you hire for that one time, and pay by the hour.

Gumtree is a great place to advertise for staff like this: **www.gumtree.com**

An often-overlooked resource is parents who decide that they do not want to return to traditional work once they have had children. They are an untapped pool of talent and experience and best yet, they don't want to work a 40-hour week. So if you need specialist expertise, but can't afford a full-time staff member, then consider advertising on these sites below to get help:

- www.workingmums.co.uk
- www.mumandworking.co.uk
- www.jobs4mothers.com

Years ago I was doing business consultancy work for a small training company that had lofty ambitions to grow. Upon completing the strategic plan, I recommended that they hire an experienced marketing manager. As they were still quite small then, they couldn't afford someone of the calibre and experience they needed full time. I suggested they advertise on the Working Mums' site, and they successfully hired a very experienced marketing manager with a perfect background but for only 20 hours a week. She was delighted as she was doing the work she loved, and they were happy as they had the expertise at the price they could afford.

One you have determined what support you require, you need to estimate the time required and the approximate cost. This will all be added into your financial modelling in the next chapter.

 ## Cost of staff

You need to consider how you may bring on resources so you can add these into your financial models. For each role you have identified use the following grid to estimate:

- how much time you will need them for every week
- what is the cost of their time.

Role	How many hours per week	Estimated cost of time

2 Where will you run your business?

Is your base a shop, a café or can you run it from leased offices, or even from your kitchen table? Where you run your business from will depend on what type of business you have and what sort of person you are.

If you need to be with other people to keep you motivated, then a shed in the garden is not for you, and a shared hub office space will be more to your liking. If you are a catering company making premium boardroom lunches, then you may need to consider renting a commercial kitchen close to where your customers are based. But if you are an HR consultant who works at her clients' offices, then finding a suitable space in your house to do the admin and business development from will suffice.

Like any business item, cost needs to be considered. If you do need to lease premises, consider how long the lease is for before you sign your life away. You don't want to change your mind, or outgrow the space only to be stuck in a three-year contract.

You need to consider the following when thinking about your place of work:

- **Do you see customers?** If you do, will they come to you? Think about the space you are in and the image it portrays. How easy is it for customers to find?

- **Security.** At the very least, you will have your computer, phones and other files and effects in this space. You may be arriving very early in the morning or leaving late at night. How safe is it? Would you feel comfortable leaving there at 8p.m. in the winter?

- **Storage facilities.** Even in this world of paperless offices, our accumulation of 'stuff' never seems to stop. Do you have enough storage capacity for your equipment, files, books, documents, etc?

- **Production requirements.** If you are making a product, where will it be made? If you are producing it, you need to ensure that you have enough room to make it, pack it for delivery and then store the materials needed to make it, and any excess stock. You need to have space available for drop offs and deliveries. Are there any health and safety requirements or regulatory considerations you need to factor in?

- **Infrastructure.** Infrastructure refers to phone, internet, computers, office equipment – all those items needed to physically run your business. If you are hosting webinars, you will need to check that there is easy access to high-speed, reliable internet. Or if you need more than one phone line with an answering service, can your premises provide that?

- **People.** From the research I conducted of 300 Corporate Crossovers, when asked what was the main thing they missed about not working at their jobs anymore, it wasn't the money they missed but the company of their co-workers. Leaving your job and starting up by yourself can be a lonely undertaking. If you think that you will feel isolated working on your own, then consider renting a serviced office, or joining a business club where you can work during the day with other business owners, or hiring a desk space in a shared office hub.

- **Distance from home.** If you are truly frustrated with the long commute between your office and home, then considering how close you want your new business to be located to your home will be an important factor. Or maybe you relish getting into the car for 40 minutes as a way to start your day and separate work from home life.

- **Room for growth.** If your business will be growing quickly, then factor this into your space requirements. Can you easily add in more staff, equipment or stock?

- **Expense.** How much will the premises cost, and can you get out of the lease easily if you need to? Will you be responsible for insurance, and are there any additional charges, for example, parking? You will need to add the cost of the lease to your profit forecast.

Possible business premises options:

- retail premises
- small factories in light industrial suburbs
- serviced offices
- clubs
- working hubs
- business incubators
- spare room in the house
- garden chalet, converted barn
- local café, library.

Helen from Montezuma's talks about how moving factories increased their production capacity and drove their thirst for more sales: '*The whole business was set up on a shoe string and we still have the mentality of you push every asset to its limit until you buy a new one and that's the same with the factory. We've moved production premises four times and massively expanded on this site last year so we are now in 20,000 square feet. We've got much more capacity so now we're hungry for lots more customers. There will be another leap in sales again which is amazing.*'

3 Being legal

No matter how big or small you plan to be, you need to decide at the start what your legal structure will be. This of course can be changed as you and your business change. I began as a sole trader and then moved to a limited liability company as my business grew and the tax laws changed.

The structure you choose for your business will determine the following:

- how much tax you need to pay
- how you personally deal with tax
- what forms and administration you are responsible to complete
- your personal responsibilities and protection.

This is a very important part of your business framework, as it will impact your tax liability, your personal exposure to debt and your professional standing. I would recommend that you do thorough research beyond what is written here, and seek professional advice from an accountant and a lawyer who specialise in start-ups.

For the latest information visit the UK Government website: **https://www.gov.uk/business-legal-structures/overview**

Simply, you have three options for how you can be set up as a business:

- sole trader
- limited liability company
- limited liability partnership.

Sole trader

This is the simplest way to start a business and requires little paper work. You are essentially saying you are self-employed. The key thing is that you MUST register with HMRC. They have a number you can call and register yourself as self-employed. This is a very simple step to take.

You will have to complete a tax return every year. You can also use a normal bank account and you can take on staff as a sole trader. The advantage of this is the simplicity and speed at which you can become registered.

Limited liability company

A limited liability company is a separate entity that lets your company stand on its own. The advantages of this are:

- **Protection**. It's the company, not you personally, that has to deal with legal obligations. You won't lose your house if it goes wrong.
- **Professionalism**. Being an 'Ltd' company can appear more professional. If you are targeting large corporates as customers, you may find that you need to be registered as a limited company before they will work with you.

There may also be tax advantages. You need to check with your accountant on your personal situation.

Compared with being a sole trader, there is also more complexity:

- You need to register with Companies House to obtain your Company Registration number: **http://www.companies-house.gov.uk/**
- You will also need to file your accounts annually with Companies House and register a number of documents (Memorandum of Association and Articles of Association).

You can do this all yourself, get your accountant to do it or register with a company that will do this specifically for you.

The tax position is different when you are a limited company, as you will have to do company accounts and pay corporation tax. You will become an employee of your limited company, so you will also need to pay personal income tax. Again, find a proactive accountant to work through this.

Partnership

If you are setting up with someone else, you will need to create a partnership. It is essential that you have a detailed partnership agreement from the outset. Even if you are the best of friends, sometimes business can go awry. An agreed and signed contract created when you still had the best intentions will make the separation easier if things do go wrong.

You can set up as an ordinary business partnership or a limited liability partnership. Each structure has different obligations regarding tax, your personal liability and reporting.

1. **Ordinary business partnership.** This structure is similar to two people coming together and creating a sole trader structure. You will both still be treated as self-employed from a tax perspective, and both partners will be personally responsible for the business.

2. **Limited liability partnership.** These are most often used by professional services firms such as accountants and solicitors. Partners in this arrangement are not liable for the debts of the business and their liability is limited to how much money they have invested in the business.

Again, take advice!

4 Protection

You also need to consider protecting yourself, your business and your idea. What type of insurance do you require? How will you protect your idea, your brand and your business name? Grouped together, this makes up the intellectual property of your business. If you have a particularly unique idea, process or service, you may want to protect it through registration, or a patent.

The British Library Business and IP Centre is extremely helpful here, offering substantial information and free advice. They conduct many seminars and consult widely on IP. Visit their website at **http://www.bl.uk/bipc/**

Another form of protection is a set of detailed terms and conditions for how a customer will work with you. These can be displayed on your website, as part of your proposal process or on your booking form.

Natalie from Miss Ballooniverse describes how her terms and conditions came about: *'I've got a set of terms and conditions at the bottom of my booking form and every single thing on there is a result of something bad that happened to me in setting up a job or on a job. For instance, if there is damage to my equipment, the client that books me is liable for it. You know in any business anything that can go wrong will go wrong at some point but you just get on with it and you survive and you get stronger.'*

5 Finances

At the heart of a business is the money. You create a business to sell products and services at a higher price than what you make them for. Even for the smallest enterprise, it is essential that you have simple systems in place to track how much money is coming into the business, and how much is going out. Otherwise you are not running a business; rather it is an expensive hobby.

In the following chapters we will cover profit and loss statements and cash flow in much more detail. For your day-to-day business framework, and to supply the information that will feed your profit and loss statement, and your cash flow, you need to have systems to manage the money.

You need to consider the following:

Bank accounts

If you become registered as a limited company, you will need to set up a bank account which is linked to your company registration details. There are specific forms that your bank will ask you to complete.

If you are a sole trader, I recommend that you set up separate accounts from your personal ones, so you can keep the in and outflow of money separate to your personal expenses.

Set up a separate savings account for tax. Every time you get an invoice paid, syphon off the appropriate amount you need to cover VAT and corporation and income tax. Doing this each time you receive money means that you have a lump sum of money easily available to pay your tax with.

Invoicing

How often will you invoice your customers and when? Will it be monthly, at the end of the month or as they buy, and you invoice them the day of purchase.

And what are your invoicing terms? Do you expect to be paid immediately, on receipt of the invoice, or will you be prepared to wait for 14 or 30 days? It may be that your payment terms are dictated to you by the customer.

Tracking income and expenses

It is imperative that you keep a close eye on the money flowing through your business. You can start off with a simple Excel spreadsheet that you update every week with details of your invoices and the money you have spent. Then each week you will know very quickly if you have made a profit or a loss.

Keep all of your receipts and invoices for seven years as you will need these for the HMRC should you ever get audited.

If accounting isn't your thing, then consider outsourcing this to a bookkeeper who you send your receipts and bank statements to, as well as your invoices. They can then track the flow of the cash for you.

VAT

When your business turnover passes £79,000 (correct at time of writing, April 2014) then you must be registered for VAT. You may decide to register for VAT even if your business isn't that big in the first year. The advantage of this is that you can claim back VAT on your purchases. This can be advantageous if you have high spending levels in year 1. Visit HMRC for advice (**www. hmrc.gov.uk**).

6 Infrastructure

What do you need to enable your business to run? Infrastructure is the term for those important elements that support a business behind the scenes. Computers, wi-fi, telephones, power, water, printers, production equipment, point of sale machines, cash registers, EFT POS, etc.

Estimating infrastructure can be kept very simple! If you are planning to have a small business, where you do most of the work, then still take some time to complete this.

You need to know how much your monthly expenses will be to run your business. Because when you come to estimating your sales, you must know how much you need to sell to make a profit each month! Otherwise you risk operating your business at a loss.

At these early stages, it can take a few phone calls or a quick internet search to make some estimates, for example:

• How much will your phone bill be each month?

• Do you need to buy paper, ink or other stationery supplies?

• What about costs of room hire, postage, etc.?

If your business is more complex, then you will also need to consider staff wages, or contracting costs (hiring freelancers can be a great way to get up and running with support, but in a way that allows you to grow it with your business thus helping you manage costs as well).

Dr Kate Hersov from MediKidz, now a global business with 41 employees around the world, recounts their start-up operations: '*So when we started Kim was coming round to my house every morning at 9 a.m. and so Medikidz really started out of my living room. We got our first employee who was an assistant who would also turn up on the doorstep at 9 a.m. and we would work from my home. It was just step by step, slowly adding other employees to the company. We moved into our first office when we had five of us in the team. So in the beginning it was very slow and considered.*'

Caution

A while ago, I decided I need a dedicated virtual assistant (VA) to work on my email campaigns, my newsletters and manage my diary, and a number of other ad hoc tasks. I went through a well-known VA school in the US which had been recommended to me. I interviewed my short list of three VAs, did extensive reference checking and chose the one I thought would be perfect.

It was a disaster! She didn't do what she was asked to do within the time frame and didn't seem to understand the rhythm of the timings in my business. Stupidly I had signed a contract with an eight-week notice period, and a set number of hours to be bought each week. After a month I knew this woman was not right for me, but I was still contractually obligated to pay her for another two months. Not wanting to renege on the contract I paid up. Ouch! I learnt so much from that experience:

1. Always have a probation period of a month where either party can leave with no questions asked in case it doesn't work out.

2. Sign a contract of work and keep the notice period down to a minimum.

I am happy to say that since then, I have had the most wonderful women support me in my business, and I used my learning from the first experience to ensure I was protected next time around.

Busy woman's shortcut

If all of the legal and IP matters make you feel as if you are entering an unchartered black hole, then take advice early on. This will save you time, money and worry in the long term. Find a specialist lawyer in start-ups and IP. I recommend Off To See My Lawyer (www.offtoseemylawyer.com), a group of lawyers that specialise in working with women start-ups.

Be savvy

Over the 11 years of running my own business, I have worked mainly from clients' offices, my home office and I rented a serviced office for six months. My serviced office was a wonderful space in a busy environment with other professionals, and I did love it. However, events transpired in my personal life that meant I needed to leave it faster than I had planned. Fortunately I had signed a one-year lease with a six-month break clause, so this meant I could leave after six months with no penalty. If you do lease premises, be sure to have a contract that allows you a break clause at six months, and then onto a rolling month's notice after that.

Like me, you never know how life may impact your business.

14

How much profit will I make?

How much profit will you make? This is the question at the heart of every business. It's time to get your calculators out, as in this chapter you will be working through the following:

- working out how much you will sell
- calculating how much profit or loss you will make in the first year
- estimating your revenues and expenses for each month in the first year.

I know that one of the biggest concerns about starting your own business is whether or not it will make any money. I am a big advocate of women doing what they love, and earning what they are worth. It's important to ensure that you make the money you need and deserve from your business venture. Don't let your business become a charity.

Profit, financial targets, margins, cash flow and balance sheets are important cornerstones of any business. Yet, I know from my clients that many of them would rather have root canal work than look at a profit and loss statement, or even check their bank accounts online. To run a successful business, you must embrace the numbers and feel empowered by them! The beauty of the numbers in business is they can give you great insight into how your business is operating.

Even in smaller businesses, getting into the detail behind the numbers is important. It may be that you have too much dependence on one customer, and your business is vulnerable to their performance, or you have a hunch that you are spending too much on one area of marketing and getting little return. Knowing your numbers intimately will give you the information you need to make effective decisions to improve your business.

Before you answer the question, 'How much profit will I make?', you need to estimate the following (and the good news is, you have done most of this work already):

- What price do you see your offering at, or what will your hourly rate be (see Chapter 11)?
- What will it cost you to produce your goods (see Chapter 9)?
- What is your estimated profit per item (see Chapter 11)?
- How much you will sell (see below)?
- What are the operating costs of your business – people, infrastructure, marketing, etc. (see Chapter 13)?

As you have completed all of the calculations except for the volume you will sell, let's look at that now.

How much will you sell?

Now you have an estimate of the profit per item you will make, to understand how much money your business will actually make, you need to forecast how much you will sell in one year. Then your gross profit estimation is simply worked out by multiplying the number of units you plan to sell by the amount of gross profit per unit.

Think about how much you want to sell in the next 12 months. What will your revenue be and how many units or services will you sell? When you are creating this number it is going to be an estimate. Look back over the work you have done already and revisit your market size and value estimates. How much market share do you think you can get? How much volume will you sell? How many hours' work will you sell?

I know that in some cases, this will be an educated guess. In these cases, it is helpful to work through the following three scenarios:

1. great result
2. good result
3. mediocre result.

You can then calculate a range of options and go with the one that feels most realistic. When you estimate your targets for the year, err on the side of caution. You will be using this top line number to invest against and you want to ensure that if your forecast is not reached that you don't bring yourself into a loss-making situation. There are many ways of creating this number. How you do it will depend on your business, the industry you are in, and how detailed you want to get. Below are some options to work through:

Option 1: Basing your numbers on how much you can produce or how much work you want to do

For example, if you want to sell cakes your calculation might look like this:

- You want to sell two cakes a week.
- You will sell each cake for £20.
- Two cakes × 52 weeks = 104 cakes.
- 104 cakes × £20 = £2080.

£2080 would be your annual revenue forecast.

To take another example, if you are offering a professional service, your calculation could run as follows:

- You want to coach 20 clients.
- You sell your coaching services for £2500.
- 20 clients × £2500 = £50,000.

Your revenue goal is £50,000.

Option 2: Starting with the overall sales figure

Many of my start-up clients decide that they want to replace their last salary from their old job in their new business. This is an equally valid place to start the calculations. For example:

- You want your turnover to be £80,000.
- You have training packages you sell at £50 each, so you need to sell 1600 packages.

Option 3: Calculating the volume you will sell based on the market, the seasonality and client responses based on your research

For instance, you design a special component for hearing aids.

- From your market research, you know that there are estimated to be 10 million deaf people in the UK and 200,000 hearing aids sold each year. You are targeting the premium range of the market, which you estimate to be 15 per cent.
- Therefore, the market you are going after is 30,000 hearing aids. You estimate you could be included in 10 per cent of those.

Therefore your goal for year 1 is to sell 3000 pieces.

Profit and loss statement

It's now time to bring this all together into one key document for your business plan – the profit and loss statement.

A profit and loss statement is exactly that – a statement of how much money you will make or lose on your business. You take your revenue targets, subtract your costs, and then you will either make a profit or a loss.

You will take all of the calculations you have done so far and bring them together to estimate your profit or loss for the first year of trading.

Create your profit and loss statement

To make this as easy as possible for you – use this simple worksheet.

Sales		
Box 1	How many products or services will you sell in a year (or how many hours will you charge out)?	
Box 2	What will be the price each one sells at (or what will be your fee per hour)?	
Total (Box A)	**Box 1 multiplied by Box 2**	£
Less Cost of Goods (Box B)	Cost of buying or making the sold stock	£
Gross Profit	**Box A minus Box B**	£
Less operating expenses	Marketing and advertising costs (including printing, website, advertising, subscriptions, networking)	£
	Travel expenses	£
	Rent and utilities	£
	Telephone and internet	£
	Returned stock	£
	Insurance	£
	Wages for employees	£
	Delivery and postage	£
Total (Box C)		£
Net Profit/Loss	**Loss or profit (Box B minus Box C)**	£

Once you have the overall picture for the year, break this profit and loss statement into months. The key variable when you break down into the months will be how much you sell. If there is seasonality to your product, you may have launches planned and extra marketing activity. All of these can affect your monthly sales. Breaking your plans down by month will allow you to see how your business will ebb and flow over the year.

	Jan	Feb	Mar	Apr	May	Jun	Jul	Aug	Sep	Oct	Nov	Dec	TOTAL
How many units													
Price per unit													
Total (Box A)	£												
Less Cost of Goods (Box B)	£												
Gross Profit (Box A – Box B)	£												
Less operating expenses	£												
Marketing and advertising	£												
Travel expenses	£												
Rent and utilities	£												
Telephone and internet	£												
Returned stock	£												
Insurance	£												
Wages for employees	£												
Delivery and postage	£												
Total (Box C)	£												
Net Profit/Loss	£												

Cash flow

Now gather together all the information about infrastructure, expenditure, marketing, etc. and map it against sales to estimate your cash flow using the following chart (remember you can download the Worksheet from www.CorporateCrossovers.com/MyNewBusiness).

Cash Flow Forecast	Month 1	Month 2	Month 3	Month 4	Month 5	Month 6	Month 7	Month 8	Month 9	Month 10	Month 11	Month 12	Total
Cash Inflows													
Cash Inflows from sales inc. VAT													0
Cash Outflows													
Trade creditors and suppliers (inc. VAT)													
Wages													0
Premises													0
VAT returns													0
Assets													0
Stock													0
Bank loans and overdrafts													0
Total Cash Outflow	0	0	0	0	0	0	0	0	0	0	0	0	0
Net Cash Flow													
Opening bank balance													
Net Cash Flow	0	0	0	0	0	0	0	0	0	0	0	0	0
Closing Bank Balance	0	0	0	0	0	0	0	0	0	0	0	0	0

Caution

I appreciate that many of these figures will be estimates. Avoid the hype and reduce your risk by keeping your sales forecasts conservative. It's always much better to celebrate an overachievement of the forecast than to constantly need to bring your estimates down because they were too high.

Busy woman's shortcut

These Worksheets are available as Excel spreadsheets on my website: www.CorpropateCrossovers.com/MyNewBusiness.

Be savvy

Years ago, when I started as general manager of a large dot-com in the UK, I was going through the numbers with my finance director for the first time. On the surface, the numbers seemed fine, we were hitting our sales targets, and spend was in line with the budgets. But something didn't feel right (remember how I talked about intuition being a great business tool?)

I asked the finance director for all the details behind the numbers. And sure enough, we were hitting our sales forecast because of a large one-off deal but there was very little sales activity forecast after this. From that, I knew that we had to act fast to get more revenue coming in, or the business would be cash negative.

15

What business know-how do I need?

Running a business successfully will require you to wear any number of hats during a month, or even during the same day. Suddenly you need to know about marketing, sales, accounting, customer management, tax and so on and so on.

From this chapter you will discover:

- what essential knowledge you need to run a business successfully
- ideas to gain that knowledge or find help.

I know that when you start a business the thought of all that you don't know can be overwhelming. When we focus more on what we don't know instead of what we do, our brain can go into overdrive and we talk ourselves out of starting.

Making it this far into the book means that you are up for a new adventure, for challenge and a fresh start! The thing I love about having my own business is that each day is different – and you are constantly learning new things.

One thing I am constantly reminded of, is that no knowledge or past experience is ever wasted. You will be surprised at how often you call on past experiences to help you make decisions and complete tasks more efficiently as you move along this journey.

You will most likely have great knowledge about your chosen field or area you are going to enter into. But if you don't know much about the area you want to move into (it could be that you have done your research and you see it as a fantastic opportunity), a good idea is to find other businesses that are in a similar field to you, or in a different industry but with a similar operating model, and ask to meet the owner for a coffee so you can discover what skills they required to set up their business. The easiest way to understand what else you need to know about the business is to ask.

Business know-how falls into two areas:

1. knowledge of the core offering
2. knowledge of how to run a business.

Do a skills audit by listing all the skills you have identified as being necessary. You can then check and see what you already have, and what you need to acquire.

You probably know more than you think. Take some time to list all of your current skills and experience – both personal and professional. Don't censor them by worrying if they are unrelated, just write. Once done, then review. I know that you will already have done a lot that will support you in your new venture.

Before you start running off and signing up for courses, carefully consider these two questions:

1. Do I need to know this skill?
2. Could I find someone who is better qualified, more experienced and knows much more about this area than I could ever hope to?

When I ask myself this question my answer is accounting and bookkeeping. Yes, I know my way around a profit and loss statement and balance sheet, but it's really not my thing to spend hours creating and updating them. I would rather pay my accountant to do that, and then I can sleep at night knowing she has everything in order.

Another area that you might decide to get help with is designing websites and brochures, etc. Of course you need these items as part of your brand, but you don't necessarily have to create them yourself.

You can learn about business, and what works and what doesn't, by studying other businesses in different areas to yours. It may be that you have an interior design business, and you are struggling with how to communicate your services and process on your website. Maybe you look for other service providers like a cosmetic dentist for ideas on how to position yourself. Be open-minded and look for new sources of inspiration and ideas for your business.

Natalie, aka Miss Ballooniverse, took the time out to model herself on businesses in related fields: '*I needed to get a website, I didn't like any of the businesses who were like me, but when I looked at magicians' websites, I saw websites that were really cool, really sophisticated, and interesting. So I took the elements that I liked and applied them to mine.*'

Let's now look more closely into the six areas of knowledge that every business owner must have:

1. marketing and business development
2. sales
3. delighting your customers
4. financial awareness
5. hiring the right staff
6. leading a team.

1 Marketing and business development

I know you are a brilliant aromatherapist who enables her clients to feel well again, or a fabulous lawyer who always goes the extra mile to protect her clients, or you have the most delicious chocolate that once you try you must have more of.

But if only you and I, and your friends and family know how wonderful you are, then your business will never grow; it will always be limited to those in your circle. Marketing is essential to grow that circle, to be able to get complete strangers considering your offering instead of what they would normally choose.

To start your business and to maintain its growth, you must spend at least 20 per cent of your time doing marketing and business development type activities. Not only do you need to have current customers and clients, but you also need to ensure that you always have a stream of new ones coming through, and then more people who become aware of your offering.

An effective approach to marketing and creating a marketing plan is outlined in Chapter 12.

2 Sales

I like to think of sales as the next logical step that someone will take with you when they have walked through the Know, Like, Trust journey. You have understood their needs so well, and demonstrated that you can provide them with a solution they will love at the right price.

Of course to make your business profitable, you need to be able to sell. Some of you reading this will be silently freaking out as you imagine that you have to become like the used-car salesman who hounded you all those years ago. But sales isn't really like that. To build a long-term relationship with your customers, you need to sell in a way that you feel comfortable with, and so do they.

Passion and energy is key to selling successfully. If you have these, you will make your enthusiasm for what your are selling infectious. Talking about your offering with passion will make it much easier for someone to buy into you and what you are selling. The conversation won't seem like a sales call, but rather an interesting discussion with someone who loves to know what you do.

Eventually though, you have to ask for the order. Whether you sell face to face or from your website, you must elicit the decision to buy. The easiest way to do this is to invite your prospect to buy. This can be done in many ways. For instance, 'When would you like to buy this?', or 'When can we start?' or 'How many would you like to order?' or have an obvious 'Buy Now' button on your website.

3 Delighting your customers

Research shows it is between five and seven times more expensive to gain a new customer than to get an existing customer to buy from you again. It's cheaper in terms of time, energy and money to continue selling to existing clients than it is to get new ones.

Delighting your customer is not only a great way to ensure that you are different to the competition, but it also helps to increase the chance that they will come back for more. Another side effect of this is the increased likelihood that they will recommend you to one of their friends. Once you get a strong word of mouth reputation, it makes acquiring new customers much easier.

Delighting your customer can be as varied as all of the different types of business out there. The key to this is to listen to your customers and exceed their expectations.

How you delight your customers will depend on the following:

- what you know about your customer and what they may value
- your type of business

- how frequently you interact with them
- what feels authentic to you.

Here are some delightful customer experiences I have enjoyed:

- being sent a handwritten note after my purchase
- articles and websites sent to me in my field of interest
- an uplifting video posted on my Facebook timeline when I needed it
- an introduction to a relevant contact
- a birthday card
- free samples of a new product
- being met for coffee, with no agenda
- calling to check that my new carpet installation went smoothly
- free delivery
- no questions asked returns policy
- beautiful wrapping paper lightly sprayed with perfume
- luscious dried rose petals sprinkled over lingerie and wrapped in tissue
- my car being comprehensively valeted after the annual service
- a car rental clerk upgrading me, warning me about the toll charges on the express ways and helping me buy tolls online

When you review the above list, you will notice that most of them cost nothing but time. In our busy lives, it is those little touches that can make the biggest difference.

Luisa Gonzalez of Waggin' Tails knows why her clients keep returning: *'They keep on coming back for the service. People like to feel that they are special. We give everyone a lot of attention. My staff know the clients and their pets by name, and the clients like that. In the end they trust us with their pets.'*

4 Financial awareness

To run a business you do need to embrace the numbers. Feel empowered by them! Many business owners I meet don't know how much income they made last month, or even last year. And they have no financial targets set for the year ahead. If you don't embrace the numbers then you will end up running a very expensive hobby.

When you start out, you can manage the numbers yourself. Set aside the same time every week to do it, make it a habit and then it becomes part of what you do. I love Financial Friday – so every Friday, I will get up to date with what's coming in, and what's gone out for that week.

I do recommend that from the start you find a great accountant. Someone you can relate to, who will transform the mysteries of a profit and loss statement, VAT and tax for you. You need someone to be watching out for you, and to keep you on the right side of HMRC. Your accountant needs to be your guide and advisor. Since they won't be as closely involved in your business, they will be able to see things that maybe you miss, and give you sound advice for your business.

Whilst you can outsource the financial bookkeeping and tax etc. to the accountant or a great bookkeeper, you must still keep a close watch over it. That way, you will not have any surprises at tax time, and you will always have a feel for how the business is growing.

Cleopatra from Celtic Quest Coasteering shares her experience: *'I can't fathom anyone that could possibly succeed not knowing the numbers. Without knowing what you are making and what you need to make versus what you are spending; how can you possibly grow and succeed? I know how much I need to make in the next 30 days in order to cover this month's overheads.'*

5 Hiring the right staff

A common barrier to growth for a small business owner is hiring staff. If you want to grow your business, you will need to hire additional resources. When you have motivated, committed and self-starting staff, your business will fly. But if you don't, then staff will be a time and energy-consuming issue for you.

There is an old adage that says, 'Hire someone for aptitude, fire them for attitude.'

Whether these people are on your payroll or contractors, this saying is still relevant. In a new, small business, this is especially important. It may be that the person you wish to hire has got an impressive track record with the right skills and experience but you have a hunch that they may not share your enthusiasm for the business, or that they may not fit in.

Selecting staff with the right attitude when you are small and in high growth is critical because of the extra demands that will be placed on them in this phase of your business. They will probably be asked to work long hours, do additional tasks outside of their job description, design new processes or even be coming up with ways to sell more. The type of person that will thrive in this environment also needs to gel with you. You have to want to spend time with them and also be able to manage them.

As part of your interview process, think not only about what they can bring to the role in terms of skills and experience, but also 'how' they will be in the role.

Ask them questions about how they:

- manage change
- cope with pressure
- come up with new ideas
- deal with ambiguity
- find new solutions
- handle deadlines.

To survive in a busy start-up, these are all essential qualities.

Keren Lerner is committed to maintaining her reputation in the market place, and is dedicated to hiring staff that share her view to deliver top-quality design and functionality: 'To build our reputation in the market, I make sure we always do a good job for everyone, and that everybody in the team knows to over-deliver on a regular basis. I only hire people who have that mentality, that are very conscientious individuals who genuinely care about doing a good job, who are wanting to please clients. They're not in it just for themselves; they have pride in their work and really want to make a difference for our clients' businesses.'

6 Leading a team

Whether you employ full-time, permanent staff, virtual part-timers or somewhere in between, it will be up to you to lead them. For some, this will be an area you already have much experience in, and probably enjoy. For those new to leadership, it is a skill that can be learnt and when you are passionate about creating success, and you share that with your staff, that will go a long way towards your success.

As Dr Kate Hersov from MediKidz comments: 'You may have the best idea in the world but if you can't inspire other people to follow you, and work with you to achieve your mission, you can't do it on your own and there's no point. At the end of the day it's all about being a great leader.'

After leading many large and small teams to launch new products and businesses, and then working with teams in my role as a consultant for my clients, I know the elements needed to be an effective leader are:

1. Share your passion and excitement for the business with them!
2. Be clear on where you are going.
3. Give people the context for the direction and decisions.
4. Ensure people are clear about their roles and responsibilities, and everyone else's.

Share your passion and excitement for the business!

Passion is contagious. You know that when you are in a conversation with someone who loves what they are talking about, you become so much more engaged and interested in that conversation and person. Business is no different. Up the ante in how you demonstrate your passion for the business, your vision and your goals and that will be a real motivator for your staff.

Be clear on where you are going

You probably know where you want your business to go, and what milestones you need to achieve to get there. Share this with whoever is working with you. Once they know what the objective is, they can offer ideas and solutions to help you achieve it.

Give people the context for the direction and decisions

Sharing with your team the reasons for decisions and changes on strategy helps them to feel valued and involved in the business. They move from just feeling like an employee and start to feel like a trusted team member.

Clarify roles and responsibilities

When people know what is expected of them, they find it easier to deliver against this. Then, when they know what is expected of others in their team, they will also offer help and suggestions. You, as their leader, need to create an atmosphere and culture where idea sharing and support is the norm. Do this by leading by example.

Caution

When you are hiring staff, even virtual, contracted staff, make sure you have a contract with them. You need to ensure that your IP is protected, there is confidentiality clause in place, payment terms and hours are agreed, and roles and responsibilities clearly laid out, as well as a notice period.

Busy woman's shortcut

Carve out one day a week to work on marketing and sales. This means that you will have the time to create and implement activities to grow your business.

Be savvy

Every fortnight I have a meeting with my virtual team using the video technology of Google Hangouts. I share with them the strategy behind my decisions, the bigger picture of my thinking and also the day-to-day challenges I face. They update each other and me with what's happening in their areas. We brainstorm ideas to drive sales and for new campaigns. I find their support and ideas not only help the business but they help me enormously as well.

16

How will I fund it?

You are ready to start. You know the business structure, the resources you need to begin and how to maintain a vibrant flow of new customers. One last thing to check – how will you pay for it all?

Keep your calculator handy, as you will be estimating:

- how long it will be from now until your first sale
- when you will make a profit
- how much money you need to fund the business until a profit is made.

The first place to start assessing whether or not you need funding to start up is estimating your cash flow. Key to this is forecasting how long it will take you to make your first sale. Knowing this, and thus the process that will be undertaken to get you to this place, is a fundamental part of planning your new business.

Once you have completed your cash flow, you will have a good idea how much money your business will need to get started, and to operate in the first year. It may be that you decide to grow organically, and only spend the money as you have it in your bank accounts, or when you have an invoice ready to be paid.

Expanding in this way limits your risk by only spending when you have the cash to cover it, and investing in new staff and equipment when the guaranteed orders require the increased capacity. The other benefit of this type of growth and self-funding of the business is that you will continue to own the business yourself.

The downside is that it may hamper your growth, limit your expansion into new areas and slow your ability to seize opportunities as they open up, and surpass the competition.

Jessica Butcher and her co-founders decided to grow Blippar organically at the start, growing as the demand required it: '*We ran to catch up with demand the whole time. So throughout our growth we felt those pain points of having generated more interest than we could possibly fulfil and it hurt. It did mean asking a lot of our early starters, ourselves and our families in terms of how we delivered on the interest that we were generating.*'

Two years on, Blippar is now having serious conversations with large-scale investors: '*It has been very much more of a strategic decision to do that. We decided to bankroll the business ourselves until a point at which we could talk to the likes of people that had invested in the Twitters and Googles of this world. That just rockets you into being able to hire the right people, getting the right traction of journalist interest. It has been deliberate that we have waited until this time to have those conversations, because now we've got a proven business model and a proven track record with people around the world, so now they are interested.*'

The first sale

There is nothing like the feeling of making your first sale – it is a culmination of thinking, planning and hard work. Suddenly you have the proof that someone else thinks this is a great idea, and that they are also prepared to pay for it! It is a momentous occasion.

Knowing the process from idea to sale will help you learn:

- the patterns of production in your business
- expenditure required to make the product
- when you can expect to get paid.

For instance, if you make cakes for sale in a café, you will need to buy the raw ingredients and make the cakes, before you get paid for them by the customer. The cakes will need to go on display in the café before the customer is tempted to buy them.

However, if you are selling to large retailers who will place an order well in advance of when they need it, you may be able to hold off buying the raw ingredients until you get the order confirmed, thus reducing the risk of that expenditure.

Over time, as you become more familiar with the operations of the business and learn how to be more efficient, this process towards a sale will be refined. You will find it easier to estimate timings, how many raw materials or components you need to keep in stock and what the sales pattern will be by the month.

 ## What are all of the steps you need to take to make your very first sale?

Write down all the steps that you need to take before you receive the money for your offering. A simple way to do this is by using sticky notes. Write each step on one sticky note – you may end up with 20 or more sticky notes as you track step-by-step the detail of everything that needs to happen from idea to cash in your bank. Finally, line up all the sticky notes in the order in which they need to be done and put a time frame to them.

For example, imagine a jewellery designer starting a business, creating jewellery that that is to be sold through shops and also directly on a website.

Below is a timeline from idea to cash in the bank.

Activity	Time before sale
Build website	Minus 20 weeks from sale
Select most favourable retailers	Minus 16 weeks from sale
Find out buyer details	Minus 15 weeks from sale
Make appointments to sell range	Minus 12 weeks from sale
Design jewellery	Minus 12 weeks from sale
Get feedback and refine	Minus 10 weeks from sale
Source components	Minus 9 weeks from sale
Take photos of prototype	Minus 8 weeks from sale
Show prototype to retailers	Minus 7 weeks from sale
Start taking retail orders	Minus 7 weeks from sale
Components arrive	Minus 6 weeks from sale
Start producing jewellery	Minus 5 weeks from sale
Put photo and buy now button on website	Minus 1 week from sale
Social media new designs	Minus 1 week from sale
Ship to retailer	0 weeks – SALE!
Invoice retailer	0 weeks – SALE!
End user starts to buy	Plus 1 week after sale
Receive payment from retailer	Plus 6 weeks after sale

From this example of creating and selling jewellery to a retailer and on a website for the first time, it will take 26 weeks for the jeweller to be paid.

In this example, the time frames are extended as the entrepreneur has to create the website, research buyers and start setting appointments. For her next range, much of this work will not need to be repeated, thus truncating her lead times.

To consider another example, for a service business such as coaching, the process may look like this:

Activity	Time before sale
Complete training	Minus 7 weeks from sale
Print business cards	Minus 6 weeks from sale
Start networking	Minus 5 weeks from sale
Set appointments to discuss coaching with prospects	Minus 4 weeks from sale
Agree pricing and terms	Minus 2 week from sale
Start coaching	0 weeks – SALE!
Invoice	0 weeks – SALE!
Receive payment	Plus 4 weeks after sale

In reality, it may take you longer to get prospects and close them to become clients, but in professional services the lead time to the sale may be much shorter than when you are producing an item.

The big caveat to this is when your target market is large corporates. The sales process into them can be complex, involving many meetings with a range of decision makers and influencers.

 ## How long until your first sale?

Use this Worksheet to work back from your first sale, and calculate what you need to have done to get your business to the point the sale is made.

Plan back from the moment the sale is made to all of the steps that need to be done from now.

The stages might include designing the product, finding suppliers, making it, finding retailers, designing a website – whatever it is, include each stage in your process. Even consider using sticky notes (see above) to capture one task on one piece of paper. Then line them all up in order and assign dates. This will give you a great understanding of the process involved in you getting your first sale.

Actvity	Time before sale

Cash flow

The piece of information that will determine whether or not you need funding, and how much, will be your cash flow. Cash flow is simply that, how the cash flows in and out of your business, and how much cash you have at any point in time (see the cash flow chart in Chapter 14).

A healthy cash flow is essential for any business, big or small. If the business runs out of money, it will be impossible to pay suppliers. You may have to get other short-term finance which may be expensive and it could become a very difficult time for you to trade out of.

To avoid this happening, you need to estimate your future cash flow. This way, you can be sure that your business has enough cash to pay its way, and you can keep growing.

This is set out like a profit and loss forecast but instead of showing when a sale is made you put in the amounts when the bill is paid. Like a profit and loss statement, there are two parts – cash in and cash out!

Cash IN

This is the moment your business receives cash in from a customer. If you get paid in cash at the moment you make that sale (as in a retail business), then you would put that payment in the same month.

However, if you invoice in one month and get paid 30 days later, then you would not enter that payment until the month it was paid and in your bank account.

Cash OUT

This is the day the money leaves your account to pay for your supplies and operating expenses. You also need to include capital expenditure here, which is for the full cost of any equipment, computers, cameras, machinery, vehicles, etc. that you purchase to run your business. You need to include the full cost you pay for them, and when you pay.

Then there should be lines for your opening balance cash inflow and then closing balance. At month 1, the cash balance is zero.

The cash inflow/outflow is total income minus total expenditure.

The closing balance is the opening balance plus the cash inflow/outflow.

Chances are very high that you will have negative cash flow in the first few months as you invest in your business to get it started. How much that negative cash flow is, is how much you will need to find to fund the start-up of your business.

Funding options

If you require capital to start up, or ongoing funding as your business develops, you will have to work out your funding options. There are many types of financing available. The best type of funding for you will depend on:

- your current circumstances
- your risk profile
- your business type and industry
- how much you require
- the time frame of borrowing
- your business projections
- whether you are prepared to use personal assets (e.g. house) for security
- whether you are willing to offer shares in your company.

> Tiffany London recounts how she funded her start-up: *'I had no money when I started the business and it didn't deter me in any way. The first money that we spent was buying stock, and we used our credit cards. We made a very small profit in our first year.'*

There are many financing options available:

- **Debt**. This is simply borrowing money. However, for how long, from whom and for what can greatly impact your business's ability to succeed. You can borrow from your friends, family, bank or other financial institutions. Debt should be used for start-up costs and buying assets including stock. Borrowing to fund ongoing expenses is generally a sign your business is not performing well.

- **Equity**. This is where you sell a portion or share of your business for cash. This could be to yourself, your friends or family, an 'angel' investor (see below), venture capitalists or private equity companies. You might also try **crowdsourcing**, which utilises the internet to reach a large audience of potential investors for small amounts of investment per investor.

- Essentially all these options amount to the same thing. That is you convincing an individual or group that YOU can build a business with their money such that they will get five to twenty times as much back in a defined time – usually within three to five years.

- **Sales**. Financing through sales (or cash flow) generally falls into three categories:
  - taking either the full sale or a sizable deposit upon an order being placed to fund costs in fulfilling the order
  - selling invoices at a discount to companies who specialise in this area (thus you get the cash from the sale less the margin taken by the invoice buyer, immediately the customer ultimately pays the face value to the invoice buyer)
  - negotiating credit arrangement with your bank based on sales orders.

- **Your customers**. Having customers pay you before delivering your product or service assures your cash flow and eliminates risk of defaults.

- **You**. In the vast majority of cases you will be providing the finance for your start-up. If you are the only shareholder and director in the business this is straightforward. However money you put into a partnership or limited company passes from your control to the entity you are investing in.

- **Friends and family.** Very often friends and family are the first option to consider after yourself. While it might seem an easy option, it is important to set out a written agreement so that both parties know what is expected. Invariably whether your business does well or struggles, the perception of who is owed what can divide the closest friends or family members.

- **Leasing, hire purchase, sale and lease back**. These are all common ways of financing where large assets are required. For example, a van, cooking equipment, computers or machinery.

- **Bank overdraft**. This is a credit facility from your bank. It is often flexible and can be arranged at very short notice. But it may have a higher interest rate than a traditional loan.

- **Bank loan**. This is credit from the bank, in which you have agreed to borrow a set amount of money and to pay it back in specific payments over an agreed period.

- **Grants**. These are an amount of money given to a business for a specific purpose. You do not need to pay these back. There is always an application process. They can be provided by charities, local councils or the government.

- **Equity finance.** Also known as investment finance, this involves selling part of your business ('shares') to an investor. The investor will take a share of any profits or losses that the company makes.

- **Angel investors**. These are individuals who decide to make investments in early-stage businesses for a share of the business.

It is imperative that you get advice you trust in this area. It may be that you consult with several experts before you form an opinion about what options are best for you.

Funding resources:

- www.eisa.org.uk – Enterprise Investment Scheme
- www.grantfinder.co.uk – find grants and soft loans
- www.j4b.co.uk – more grants
- www.princes-trust.org.uk
- www.venturesite.co.uk – another website for business angels
- www.kickstarter.com – a crowdfunding site
- www.indiegogo.com – a crowdfunding site for creative projects
- www.crowdfunder.com – connects investors and entrepreneurs
- www.crowdcube.com – UK-based crowdfunding site
- www.spacehive.com – UK-based crowdfunding site
- www.seedrs.com – UK equity-based crowdfunding site
- www.crowdbank.com – UK equity-based crowdfunding site

Be savvy

In your set-up, spend only what you need to. Keep your expenditure low. This is referred to as bootstrapping. For instance, if you need furniture, find second-hand, look to share resources with other business owners and consider what you can do yourself.

Caution

Before you take on any funding, seek advice. Spend time with your accountant and/or lawyer to understand the implications of your funding. And be especially clear on the risks involved if you fail to pay it back or meet the growth targets.

Busy woman's shortcut

At the start of your business journey, you may not be considering funding. It may be required later if you decide you want to expand and need the extra funds to achieve this. You will need robust financial documentation to prove that your business is what you say it is. Keep thorough records from the start and create systems that will ensure all the information is collected and analysed correctly.

5

How do I do it all?

By now you will have the clarity, confidence and commitment to start your business. You have a good estimate of what you will make, who will buy your offering and how you will reach them. Fantastic!

Yet you may still be wondering if you can really do it. How will you manage your current life and still find time to pour your heart and soul into your new venture? The final part of my book will walk you through the emotional side of your start-up journey, and give you practical tips on how to flourish!

17

Chapter

What does starting up on your own feel like?

I have often thought that starting your own business is like a personal development programme that you are completely unprepared for. You will experience peaks, troughs, fear, elation and everything in between.

In this chapter you will discover:

- what the start-up journey feels like
- four strategies to make the transition as smooth as possible.

There are times when I have wanted to stop being self-employed and go back to the seeming comfort of corporate life and be paid a salary and work regular hours. But I know that I am dreaming as I love the freedom, flexibility and control that having my own business affords me. I know that if things aren't going my way, then it's completely up to me to make a change to get a different result.

That total and utter responsibility for your outcomes can be immensely fulfilling or downright scary. It just depends on what day of the week you ask an entrepreneur.

When I wrote my book *Corporate Crossovers: When it's Time to Leave the Office* after speaking in-depth to 50 Corporate Crossovers, and from my own coaching work of many years, I devised this model of what it feels like to start your own business, based on Elisabeth Kubler-Ross's well-known five stages of grief model.

Whether you have left your job, or decided to start your own business after a period of not working, this model will represent how you will feel during the transition.

Corporate Crossovers Transition Model

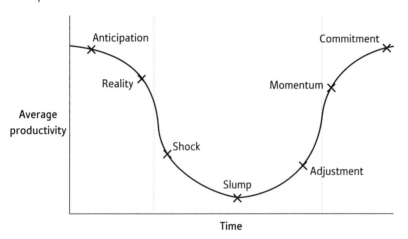

There are seven phases in the Corporate Crossover Transition Model (taken from *Corporate Crossovers: When it's Time to Leave the Office*, Momentum Coaching Change Management, 2014). From my own experience and that of my clients, everyone goes through this model at a different pace. Some phases are more extreme than others; you may linger longer in some phases. Determinants for the journey through the transition are:

- your natural temperament
- the reason why you set up the business

- the amount and depth of preparation you did
- how large your financial safety net is.

Phase 1: Anticipation

The first phase of the transition is one of anticipation. You feel hopeful and optimistic. You are about to embark on an exciting opportunity. You are fuelled by the feeling that at last you are doing it, especially if you have been a long time in the planning.

As the days and weeks go by your optimism and eager anticipation start to fade and confusion, doubt and worry may set in. Confusion about how to prioritise your time. Doubt over whether you have made the right decision. Worry about whether it will work.

Phase 2: Reality

That initial glow of enthusiasm has worn off. The novelty has been replaced by a long 'to do' list. There are many decisions to make, precious money to invest and people to start calling. Doubt creeps in as you wonder how you will possibly get everything done and start trading to make money.

You start to miss your old way of life and with this, you begin to question whether or not this was such a good idea. The sense of responsibility that the success of the business is completely in your hands starts to set in.

Phase 3: Shock

As the reality sets in, so does more work, more isolation and more doubt. The fear creeps in as you constantly stretch and operate outside of your comfort zone to do all that needs to be done. Sales don't happen as fast as you would like and the business plan looks like a fantasy.

You are not sure about how to talk about what you do, and what your identity is anymore. You find it hard to 'sell' yourself, your business, as it all seems too close to you. You can get stuck in the minutiae of setting up the business. Working in this detail saps your energy.

Phase 4: Slump

If the shock continues, you will start to enter the slump. Low energy, low motivation and an even bigger questioning if all the long hours for less money are really worth it. You may be fed up with the red tape or maybe you are still searching for funding or that big customer.

You feel isolated as you are working hard by yourself to get the business moving. This is the time where you may start to ponder if getting a job again is an easier option. Should you 'get real, and get a job'? This stage represents the greatest risk of you returning to being an employee again.

You also enter a period of acceptance. You accept that this is the choice you have made. And that this is how your situation will remain if you continue with questioning your decision. The acceptance moves you into the adjustment phase.

Phase 5: Adjustment

In this phase, optimism returns and your energy rises. The vision you have of your business being successful becomes tantalisingly real again. You start to get more wins, and you feel things are finally moving in the right direction.

You know how to talk about what you do and you do this with pride as you build your new identity. Those difficult start-up problems have been solved, and you are feeling more confident about your income stream.

Your days and weeks have more rhythm to them, which supports you. There is a structure to your time that works. You and your business start to receive positive feedback and your confidence grows.

Phase 6: Momentum

You have adjusted to your new life and fully reconciled with your decision to leave your job. Your feeling of isolation has subsided as you become an active networker, proactively seeking opportunities and connections.

Financially you have adjusted to the peaks and troughs of income flow and you are feeling confident that your sales pipeline is healthy. You have also found the right support, realising that you don't have to do it all yourself, nor do you have to find all the answers yourself.

You can start to see a direct impact between your effort and the success of your business. This enhances your confidence and builds your momentum. You start to talk about your business more enthusiastically; the vision you dreamt of becomes even closer to being attained.

Phase 7: Commitment

The business flows with grace and ease. You continue to get brilliant feedback and you are feeling much more positive about the future. Your knowledge of the business has grown and you understand more about how the business ticks; what levers you need to pull to reduce costs, increase sales, manage profitability. You feel a great deal of pride in your offering and can see the potential of it more clearly than ever before. Your identity and your business are closely meshed. You can't ever imagine going back to your old life.

What I discovered after delivering a talk about this model to a group of women art dealers in London, is that the feelings described in this model can occur even if you have been in business for 20 years. A member of my audience described her experience after repositioning her business to represent a different type of artist to what she had done previously. She felt like she was starting the business all over again.

Four strategies to smooth the transition

You will go through transition when you start your business, and there are four strategies you can adopt to try to shorten and smooth the transition phases.

1 Strong vision

Creating a strong vision of what you want your business to be and why you are creating it are essential to moving through the model. I like to think of a strong vision as the magnet that will 'pull' you through the phases faster.

A strong vision will lift your spirits when you view it, and will remind you of why you started the business in the first place. You may recall we did the work on vision boards in Chapter 4. These are great to capture your dreams and aspirations for the business and the life you wish to create from this. If you haven't created a strong vision, then revisit Chapter 4 for some ideas on how to do it.

Another way to create a strong vision is to invent a vision statement for yourself. In this you would describe what you have created and how you feel about it. For instance, 'I am running a successful consulting business, where work flows in easily and I have the spare time and energy to spend as I wish.'

2 Updating your identity

When we start our own business, how we describe ourselves changes. We are no longer an 'x' employee at a 'y' company, or a full-time stay-at-home mum, but now something different. And this description is not just about what we do on the outside but also who we are becoming on the inside.

To do this, set some time aside to ponder who you are now. This may seem like a facile exercise but I want you to go deep. Go beyond a title, or a description of what you do. I want you to deeply consider the difference you make and the impact you have on your customers.

So, if you were a marketing manager for Walkers Crisps, and that was your identity for many years, and before that possibly a junior marketer at a different food company, and now you are considering starting up a high-end, allergy-free cake brand, your strongest identity will be that of a food marketing expert, as that is the role you have had the longest. But now, you create delicious cakes that are free of ingredients that cause allergy sufferers grief. Your identity is more than just a cake baker, you are a person who allows those with food limitations to enjoy all the delicious cakes they please. You enhance their lives by giving them choices that were previously unavailable.

 ## Updating your identity

Start thinking about your new identity by answering the following questions.

1. How do you talk about yourself now?
2. What is your business idea and the problem it solves? How would you describe yourself as the creator of that business?

3 Knowing what success really looks like

Have you defined success for yourself as a new business owner? Your constructs of success have probably changed, especially when you made the decision to start up. It means that what success was for you before, may no longer be relevant. If you have left your job and you defined success by the external measures so often foisted upon us in an organisation (title, size of team, salary, etc.), when you leave and set up by yourself, these success criteria may no longer apply.

Or if you have decided to no longer be the full-time care giver, then how you define success will be different too.

Take some time to think about what success is for you now.

Update your success criteria!

Step 1: Acknowledge the past

When you had a job how did you define success then? Write down 10 elements that were important to you and made you think you were succeeding.

Here are some thought starters:

- impact on the bottom line
- working with a large team on important projects
- doing something that made a tangible difference to people
- salary
- business class travel
- meeting with senior decision makers
- large budgets
- feeling respected
- working for a great brand
- job title.

Step 2: What's precious now?

What is most precious to you now? How do you want to spend your time and your energy? What are your dearest values? Write down between five and ten areas that are key to you now.

The following are some ideas to help you along:

- independence
- feeling like I make a difference
- family
- variety
- freedom
- financial security
- time with children
- state of mind

- time to pursue other interests beyond work
- working with people I like
- creativity
- opportunity
- growth
- financial success.

Step 3: Take a measure

Reflect on your 'precious now' list that you created in Step 2. How much is your current work and personal life reflecting those values?

Could this be success for you now? How does it compare to your past criteria of success? What comes up for you when you read it and think about the two lists?

As we go through our life we are constantly evolving. By checking in and updating our values and our view of success before major change eases the pain of transition, we judge ourselves and our choices more compassionately. Increased self-awareness buffers us from our harshest critic – ourselves.

4 Acknowledging that it happens – normalising

This may sound a little odd but sometimes acknowledging that we will go through this transition helps. This is called 'normalising'. When you see a model or phenomena that describes what you are going through, suddenly you feel normal, as you realise that you are not the only one going through this.

Be aware of how you are feeling, acknowledge it and try not to let it drag you down if you are going through a dip. All things pass. Go back to your vision board and remind yourself of the big reason why you started this business.

Caution

Fear, frustration and faltering are all normal emotions when you start up. You are stretched. Remember there are phases you will go through, and each one will pass. When you go through these phases ensure you surround yourself with people who will support and inspire you.

Busy woman's shortcut

As reluctant as I am to put in a shortcut for this transition, I know that when you create a magnificent vision, tangible goals and a plan to achieve them, this is the best way to make the transition shallower, quicker and easier.

Be savvy

If you have a day where your motivation is fleeting and you just can't work, stop. Accept that the energy isn't there and go and do something you enjoy. I know that by doing this, the following day you will be more inspired and motivated. Things will be completed with ease and grace.

18

How do I sustain my commitment?

You are on your way. Idea refined, researched and ready to go. Numbers crunched and profit figures looking plausible. It's time to think about how you keep going through all the ups and downs that your own business will invariably throw at you.

In this chapter you will discover:

- simple and effective tools to keep your motivation high
- why tracking your business daily is essential to success
- what my favourite sound is in the world, and how it relates to business.

With no boss, or organisational structure to ensure you deliver your work on time, how do you keep motivated and working towards your goals? To be successful in your own business, your motivation and self-discipline to do the work you need to, must be ever present. All fine in theory but even the most focused, task-driven business owners will share with you times when it was all too much, and they faltered.

Sustaining your motivation and commitment to the business can be easy at times and then almost impossible at others. Accept this. Accept that you are human and there will be times when you think your business is fun, exhilarating and energising, and other times when you think the exact opposite.

Jane from Jane Plan shares her ride: *'There's part of me that absolutely loves this and there's a part of me that thinks it's quite overwhelming a lot of the time. If you have a job, I don't think you have the extremes as in your own business. You don't have that huge high but at the same time you don't have that big low either. A job is a much more constant thing so it's learning to deal with the ebb and the flow of the business that's hard.'*

Sustain your commitment by using these eight suggestions below:

Look at your vision board daily

Remember in Chapter 4 you created a fabulous vision for your business? It is an evocative and inspirational representation of how you want your business to be. A daily view of the board will reconnect you with your excitement and aspiration about the business and feed your energy. With each repeated view, you are strengthening that neural pathway associated with achieving your business vision.

If you have decided that you are creating a legacy business, then that too will sustain your commitment. You want to be around for a long time, not just until your interest wanes.

Helen from Montezuma's explains: *'What you don't appreciate is when you set up a business you fall in love with it. It is a bit like a child that's now growing into a petulant teenager. We just don't want to part with it, which is a nice position to be in. Now we've got children we talk about the future a lot more. Our plans for the business are very much for a long-term family business. If one of our girls wanted to come into the business at some point, that would be amazing. Obviously, that's quite a way off, but Montezuma's will hopefully be around in 10, 20, 50 years' time.'*

Find an accountability buddy

Perhaps you are one of those people who find it easy to plan and write 'to do' lists, but then struggle to bring the plan to life or to actually do the tasks on the list. This might be because those activities require you to do something that you feel scared about or uncomfortable with.

Sometimes it is easier to procrastinate, to do a simpler task and avoid that discomfort. Often those tasks we avoid are the very ones that will move our business to the next level. And yet we find ways not to do them.

Finding an accountability buddy will help you manage this unhelpful tendency. An accountability buddy is simply that, a friend who will keep you accountable to do what you said you would do.

It is important to choose someone whom you respect, and in some way, don't want to disappoint. You need to have that feeling with them, so you feel compelled to complete your tasks in between your calls.

Once you have found the right person, set up a weekly call to review each other's tasks and commitments. Knowing that you have a call with someone on a certain day will motivate you to get those tasks you committed to done.

Track your progress

Life is busy. So busy we can forget how far we have come. Tracking the progress in your business against your goals will remind you how far you have come and what success you have had.

When you are going on a journey, you set your destination and along the way you check how close you are to getting there. Running your business is no different. You have set the destination with your goals, created the route with your plan and now you need to check how far you have come.

Tracking your business progress against a set of metrics representing your goals, will enable you to feel in control. You will have a sense of what's worked and what hasn't in building your business. Your confidence will grow as you get to understand more about how your business works.

Track the following metrics weekly:

- income
- expenses
- website traffic
- sales pipeline.

Remember why you will succeed

When we are constantly stretching ourselves out of our comfort zone, we can wonder if we will ever succeed. We don't have people telling us how well we are doing or giving us feedback, so we need to rely on ourselves.

You need to bolster yourself and have something to tap that you can look at if your spirits are flagging. Spend some time creating this list.

Ten reasons why you will succeed at this business

Make a list of the 10 reasons why your business will succeed. These may range from relevant work experience to your tenacity or other personal qualities. They can also include things you have done in your personal life. Then, if you should hit a point that makes you feel despondent about your abilities, reach for this list and refresh your self-belief.

Get the love

Customer love is a two-way street. Yes, it starts with you delighting your customers, but it finishes with you getting wonderful feedback from your happy clients.

Create a customer love file, on your computer or buy a physical file. Then each time you receive some positive feedback, take it and place it in the file.

This will serve two purposes:

- when you need to be reminded of the great work you do, it is there right in front of you
- you will have an easy way to find customer testimonials should you need them for your website or other promotional material.

Justine Roberts from Mumsnet recounts how her customer feedback kept her going in the early days: '*Although it was proving very hard to make it a financially viable business, it very quickly became a useful thing for our readers. I would receive emails from people saying, "This is a life saver", "I've met such wonderful people, thank you so much". We would get those emails every week, and I always thought, if something is this useful and this loved, it has got to eventually make itself pay, surely. So I clung on to that hope.*'

Three daily wins

When we reflect on the day that has passed, it is more common for us to remember what we haven't done, what hasn't gone right and our issues than it is to reflect on all of the positive things that have happened that day. Consequently, we end the day feeling pressured, and anxious about the problems we have to solve.

Imagine if you ended the day remembering things that had gone well, and that you had completed? You would finish work feeling buoyed about what had gone well, content that you had done some work and even a little excited about the next day.

A simple exercise to do at the end of each day is to take five minutes and write down three things that have gone well for you. They can be big or small. It may be you landed a big client you had been working on for a while, or you updated your LinkedIn profile.

Finishing the day thinking of what has gone well will start to make you more optimistic. This is because as you get into the habit of finishing each day looking for what has gone well, over time you will naturally start to ask yourself during the day, 'Is this something I can add to my list?' Thus turning your mind into looking for the positive in the moment.

Support

Starting up your new business can feel like a lonely adventure at times. You are so busy that time to maintain your friendships slips away as you spend what precious spare time you have with your family.

From my survey of 300 Corporate Crossovers, the main thing they missed about their job wasn't the money, it was their old work mates. They felt lonely starting up by themselves, having no one in their office to bounce ideas off or to share successes or frustrations with.

There will also be times when you may want to bounce an idea off someone, or try out a new approach or strategy.

There is a range of support options for you as a business owner. Give them all a try, as some you will really like, and others not quite so much. Keep an open mind.

Support options:

- networking groups
- Facebook groups to stay in touch
- a coach mentor to help you through it
- Chambers of Commerce
- your accountant.

Luisa Gonzalez counts her family and self-belief as a key source of her support: '*I think that I have an amazing family as last year I was really having a bad moment and my Mum and Dad flew from Venezuela to give me support. Everyone in the family is "keep going, keep going". I think it's also the belief that it is going to work. I mean, that's the main thing. If you don't believe in what you are doing, that's the end. As long as you believe in what you are doing you can take anything.*'

As Catherine Watkin says: '*One of my biggest supports is other women who are running their businesses and are going through the same stuff that I am. They understand me and inspire me, and are inspired by me. It's one of the things I like most about being in business for myself. Because there are a lot of days it's really, really tough but one of the things I like the most is being part of this interconnected web of other women in business. It's ultimately the best thing about it all.*'

Celebrate!

I have a confession. My favourite sound in the world is not the laughter of my two children; it is the 'pop' of the cork being released from a bottle of champagne.

'Pop.'

That wonderful sound conjures up celebration, conviviality and a sense of occasion.

Celebrating our achievements and successes, allows us to acknowledge what we have done, and to burn that feeling of achievement and success into our brains.

Too often, we have moved onto the next project or the next goal without pausing to celebrate our achievement. Time rushes by, and what we have done gets blurred. We forget the great things we have done, and how we stretched ourselves to achieve them.

Actively remembering our successes and feeling successful, enables us to build more success! It provides you fuel to keep going forward.

Each time you achieve a milestone, make sure you mark it with a celebration.

Be savvy

Create a system to collect testimonials and feedback from customers. Whether you send them an email with questions to prompt a testimonial, or ask for a LinkedIn referral, do it as soon as they have finished using your offering. That way, the experience you gave them is fresh in their mind, and they will be more keen to do it.

Caution

One of my favourite quotes is from Jim Rohn, a personal development guru from the US: 'You are the average of the five people you spend the most time with.' Consciously choose to spend your time with people who motivate, support and inspire you to live your full potential.

Busy woman's shortcut

Social media is a great way to stay connected and build international connections and drive traffic to your website. But it can also be a wonderful tool to aid procrastination. Create two 15-minute time slots in your day, at 10 a.m. and 5 p.m., to 'do' your social media. That way you will avoid falling into the time suck trap.

19

How do I manage my life as well as my business?

Every day I am reminded of how intertwined our personal and business lives are. Now you have done the work in the business planning, it's time to create some strategies for success.

In this chapter you will start to consider:

- how to manage the potentially conflicting demands on your time
- creating a working routine that suits you
- the different types of support you may need and how to find them.

Starting a business will take over your life, if you let it. A common trait of start-up entrepreneurs is that many of them haven't had a holiday for at least three years, and they often work most weekends. They tell me it doesn't feel like work, because they love it so much, but I know that this level of work can take its toll on relationships and health.

Go back to Chapter 1 and review how you wanted your life to be as a result of starting your business. I would be pretty sure that you didn't write anything in that description that included working seven days a week for twelve months of the year.

As addictive as starting your own business can be, you must have some down time, not only to rejuvenate and reenergise for the next stint of work, but also to ensure that you have a balanced perspective on the work you are doing.

Taking time out feeds your creativity, exposes you to new ideas and freshens your thinking.

When you think about managing your life, you may also have additional responsibilities in your home life. Whether it is children, elderly parents or something else, these will also require your time and attention. With some thought and planning, you can create a balanced life, in the way you want it.

Identify your priorities

What do you really want now you have begun your journey as a business owner? Knowing this will allow you to make quick decisions about how to use that most precious resource, your time.

Take some time now and select your priorities. I recommend you only have two at the most. Below are a few ideas to get your thinking started, and even though they may not align to what you want, they will give you an idea of how to create priorities.

Possible priorities:
- to earn as much money in my business as I did in my last job
- to be able to fund the children's childcare easily
- to be with my elderly parents when they need me
- to spend time with the kids when I want to
- to keep my exercise programme going
- to have time to spend with my friends during the week
- to work only between nine and five
- to create a business I can sell in five years.

Being extremely clear on your priorities will enable you to make decisions faster about whether or not to do something. You will also be able to review quickly how on track you are in aligning to them.

Priorities also help to reduce any guilt you may be feeling: the guilt that you can't be in two places at once, or guilt that you may not be doing anything well enough. When you are clear on your priorities, that helps let that guilt go.

Know what 'good enough' is

It is easy to feel like you are doing a mediocre job at everything, being a business owner, a mum, a daughter, a wife, partner, friend or whatever when you are constantly feeling torn and needing to manage conflicting priorities. This feeling of never doing well enough can eat away at our confidence and sap our motivation. We can become lethargic as we accept that we never do anything well enough, so why bother trying.

Ugh! An easy way to overcome this is to define what 'good enough' is. Define it, write it down and make it tangible. This will then be a benchmark that won't keep moving, it can be something you can objectively and fairly measure yourself against.

My hunch is that we tend to judge ourselves and our commitment levels quite harshly. Our inner critic kicks in and loves to berate us on what we haven't done. Be kind to yourself and set your standards for 'good enough' and use those as your measure.

Is it good enough to:

- answer emails within 48 hours instead of the same business day
- leave the breakfast dishes until dinner time so you start work quickly in the morning
- buy ready meals for a casual kitchen supper instead of hosting a full dinner party
- do the grocery shopping online and save at least two hours a week

Start to ease up on yourself, and you will reduce the pressure.

Create goals and a plan to achieve them

When you have no goal for your business and no plan, you can feel lost, overwhelmed and stuck. It can be hard to get motivated as you question what the point of it is. Especially if you feel torn between conflicting priorities.

Avoid this scenario by creating a simple operating plan for your business. This will give you more focus, as you will know where you are going and how you will get there.

You will feel more motivated and liberated as the path is laid out clearly for you to execute against. Try this simple approach:

- Create a goal to achieve for the next three months.
- Identify the actions you need to do to achieve it.
- Group these actions into weekly tasks, and diarise them.

This will help you get into focused action.

Creating boundaries around your work

Act like you are working for someone else, and this will transform how you spend your time. Start setting boundaries and creating rituals to mark the start and end of each working day. This reduces the blending of your work and personal time.

Start work at the same time every day

When you used to work for someone else you had to turn up for a certain start time each day. Start making boundaries between your personal and work life by choosing a time to 'start work'. Start work at the same time every day, and this will help you have a clear delineation between personal time and work time.

When you are at work, work

Once you have your time chosen to 'start work', then work. Discipline yourself to focus. Don't be tempted to put a load of washing on, or quickly do the vacuuming. If you were working in an office, you wouldn't be doing this.

Start to respect your business by working during your working time.

Stop work at the same time every day

In the same way that you create a 'start work' time, choose a time to 'end the day'. And end the day. No sneaking back to check email after dinner or when the kids have gone to bed, but truly commit to making the end of the working day the end. Reclaim your personal time by creating boundaries between work and personal time.

Be work ready

Dress for work

When you get ready for work when you have a job, your mindset shifts. You feel like you are getting into work mode as you put your work clothes on. It can be tempting when you work for yourself to work in your pajamas, but how would you feel if a client dropped by unexpectedly? Put your 'work' mindset on in the morning by dressing as if you were seeing clients that day.

Now you have created boundaries around your work time, use them. All work and no play not only makes us dull but it hampers creativity, we lose our perspective on our problems and work, and frankly we become mono-dimensional and boring. I am sure this wasn't in the description of the life you wanted to create.

Create a workspace you love

Where you work will be a significant determinant in how successful and productive you feel. Create a workspace that feels inviting, calm and efficient. Respect your business and yourself. Create a beautiful working environment, with enough space for you and your tools, books and files – one you would feel proud to show clients around.

Take some time to imagine the ideal working space for you. Create a vision board of the elements you would love. Do you crave to be surrounded by white, clear spaces and a zen-like atmosphere? Or do you prefer colour and a high-energy environment?

Creating your ideal workspace will help you look forward to your day and means that you actually enjoy spending time where you work. Spend some money on making it desirable. Many stationery shops and large furniture stores have a huge range of colourful office supplies. Indulge yourself and invest in some pieces that bring your look together.

Realigning roles in the home

If you choose to work from home, suddenly you may appear to be more available to do more household tasks. Whether you or your partner place this expectation onto you, ask yourself, 'Is this really what I want?'

You started a business and you need to remember that you are working. Business in its start-up phase requires even more energy than when it has been running for a while, so you need to focus your efforts to move towards your goals, not be tempted to quickly put a load of washing on while you are working.

To avoid other people assuming you will do more of the work around the house, then you must have a discussion about roles and responsibilities. I know this sounds rather business-like, but in the same way that you developed a list of tasks and then roles for your new business, take the time to that for the running of your home.

In this period of flux, it may be a perfect opportunity to reassign tasks and responsibilities to different household members.

Where is your value?

We often do things because we always have. If you are finding that your free time is being consumed by your business or you simply do not have the energy to do the cleaning at the weekend then outsource it. I am an advocate of outsourcing all lesser value and low cost tasks to a cheaper resource – in my business and in my home.

When you run your business, your time is precious and you need to have space to renew and replenish your energy.

As a business owner your time has a value to it, just like every other resource in your business. I have a detailed calculation that estimates that the cost per hour of a business owner's time to the business if they wish to have annual revenue of £100,000 is £123.

The calculation, detailed below, shows how you can drill down to what an hour of your time costs your business if you want to earn £100,000 working five days a week, seven hours a day.

It does this by:

- estimating how many days you actually work in a year by subtracting holiday, sick days and bank holidays
- working out how many hours a day you work
- calculating how many hours a year you work
- then dividing your revenue target by the number of hours you work.

Voila! The opportunity cost of your time to your business.

How to value my time to get to £100,000	
GOAL = £100,000 Work 7 hours per day 5 days a week	
1. Total number of days in working year	5 days x 52 weeks = 260
2. Public holidays in my location	–10
3. Number of holidays	–15
4. Number of sick days	–3
5. New total of working days	232 days
6. Number of hours I work each day	7 hours
7. Number of hours per year	232 x 7 = 1624 hours
8. Revenue goal	£100,000
9. Revenue per hour	£1000,000/1624 = 61.57
10. Double-productive half the time	**123.14 per hour**

So, your time costs the business £123 per hour. This is, of course, an opportunity cost. Think of it like this, if you spend an hour on Wednesday doing the cleaning, that has cost your business £123.

Because instead of doing that, you could have spent that hour adding value to your business. For example, you could have phoned warm prospects, closed them, and thus earnt your business some revenue or planned your marketing for the next two months, or followed up with some people you met at a networking event.

Your personal time must be thought of in the same way. If you find that you are too tired at the weekend to do the housework, consider outsourcing it to a lower cost resource. Save your energy for an activity that will replenish you, or add more fuel to your creativity for work on Monday morning.

Grow your intellectual assets

Many women, when they think about starting their business, are fearful that they will not have the right skills to be a success. You will learn so much when you start your own business. However you may still feel that a skills or knowledge gap exists.

If you think this is the case, then take some time out and create a plan about what you need to learn, and how you want to feel in a particular area. Think about what you want to know in 12 months' time. What knowledge do you want to acquire, what skills do you need to master to feel confident in running your business?

Take the time to create a learning plan. Once you have identified the knowledge you want to acquire, then investigate all of the different ways of getting it. It may be online courses, face-to-face workshops, study with a mentor or a book on a specific subject. Write down all the options, cost them out and then decide when you will do them.

A word of advice from someone who has invested in many learning experiences over the years. Only do one at a time and be very clear what the benefit is for you to do this. Treat investment in learning like any other investment in your business. Be clear on what the return on investment will be before you start.

Investing in herself has paid off for Alicia: *'I've always invested in learning and training and that has been massive for me. Every time that I've invested money and time in my professional development I've always had a big shift.'*

Business support

I worked as marketing manager on Colgate toothpaste and our offices were directly over the toothpaste factory. Each week we would go downstairs and have a production meeting with the factory staff. Without fail there was always a point on the agenda about the condition of the toothpaste production machine. In my early naivety, I used to think that talking about a machine was a waste of time until it dawned on me that if it broke down, we would have no more toothpaste. And if we had no toothpaste, we couldn't sell anything to the supermarkets. Then we would not make our revenue and profit forecasts. Our business was totally dependent on that machine. Your business is totally dependent on you. You are it's most important asset, as without you, it wouldn't exist.

I believe that as business owners, we are the most important assets our business has. Yet often we don't treat ourselves like that. Your business is totally dependent on you. You must schedule in time and set aside money to nurture yourself, physically, intellectually and spiritually.

When we run our own businesses, we can feel overwhelmed by what we have to do, or unsure of what direction to go in next. We may feel as if our motivation is flagging and we need a way to be bolstered. If you find yourself in these situations, consider hiring a business coach or mentor. Every other year I have hired a coach, and in that year my business increases by at least 50 per cent. That is no coincidence. Even though I know a lot about running a business, at times I need someone else to stretch me to realise my true potential.

Moral support

Someone once said to me, 'Life is like a stool with three legs. You have a leg for work, one for friends and the last one for your partner.' Since running my own business, I think life is more like a table with four legs, and the extra leg is for my business buddies. These days I count fellow business people among my close friends. I can be completely honest with them because they 'get' what I am going through; they know how a problem in your marriage can impact your revenues because you don't have the energy to go out selling, or they know how when a big client is threatening to leave how devastating that can be and the worry it puts into your home life.

I wouldn't be where I am today without my business buddies. I recommend you find some of your own. I found mine while attending workshops and through networking groups I belong to.

'Connecting with people that are on the same path to me has been invaluable,' Alicia Cowan recollects. She goes on to say: *'There have been times where I have really struggled to put myself out there, where I have really had to face my fears and break old habits. I wouldn't have been able to do that without the support of people who were going through a similar situation as me.'*

Busy woman's shortcut

I know from first-hand experience how often my nurturing time gets cut because I am too busy to book it! Now I have my Virtual Assistant do it, so it does happen, but if you don't have a VA, take half an hour now, and book in those sessions (massage, walk with a friend, visit to an art gallery...) into your diary. Then they will have a greater chance of happening.

Taking time out for yourself with friends, is also a great way to keep your friendships alive. The old saying, 'All work and no play makes Jack a dull boy' holds equally true when you run your own business.

Be savvy

As you start up your business, take some time to think about what is the BEST routine and support structure for you. When are you most energised, motivated and creative? Is it a certain time of the day or at the start of the week? What is the routine around your work life you need to create to support you? Actively plan and create this knowing that it will allow you the best chance of success.

Caution

Time to be honest. Are you running a business, and fitting in everything else around that, or fitting your business in between other activities?

There is no right or wrong answer here, but whatever your approach, accept the reality, and create your goals and plans accordingly.

Is it possible to juggle running a business with motherhood?

Is it possible to create a successful business, be the main care-giver in the family and still have a life?

Yes.

This chapter will help you discover how you can do it all ... or those bits you choose to!

Define what 'all' is

The idea of 'having it all' is thrown about in the media so much and we are now being told that we can't have it all. I disagree. I think you can have it all if you know what your 'all' is.

So what does having it all mean to you?

From the last chapter, you will have started to define what is important in your life and business once you are up and running. This is the start of defining what you 'all' is.

This is the time to really dig deep. Try to eradicate from your mind those pictures of perfect domestic goddesses or women with a gaggle of babies making it big in the board room. Your version of 'it all' will be a personal reflection of your values and what's most important to you. What anyone else thinks here is completely irrelevant.

Revisit the priorities, values and the wonderful vision board you created in Chapter 4 to create your version of 'it all'.

Perhaps your 'all' is:

- working three days a week, meeting stimulating people in a field you are passionate about, exercising three times a week and then pursuing your hobby or sport, and having the right amount of time with your children
- working five days a week, only in school hours so you can be there for the children
- working full time, with a nanny or au pair so you can work late nights and be away for your work.

Whatever it is, it's all about what is right for you right now. I know from my own experience and that of my clients that this 'right' will change over time as your personal circumstances shift.

Write down your own version of 'having it all'.

Working at home with children

If you have decided to start your business to spend more time with the children then you must actively plan how this will work. Too often you can feel that you are doing neither role well. I have had clients share with me their feelings of guilt as they push their child on a swing in the park, whilst checking their emails on their phone. No one wins in this scenario. Not you as the mum, or you as the business owner.

Below are some suggestions to make this easier.

1. **Plan and agree your working schedule.** Create and agree a working schedule with your family. Decide the hours you will work at home – when you start, when you finish, when you break for lunch. Set these boundaries, explain them to your children and then stick to them. This sets the expectation that you will be working on this day and at this time, which makes it much easier to implement.

2. **Try cost-effective childcare options.** Consider doing childcare swaps with other working mums in your area. This is a cost-effective way to get a morning or two of free time. There may be a nanny or an au pair already working for a family in your area that has a spare morning or afternoon every week. Ask around, and that could give you that extra quiet time you need.

3. **Be an early riser.** The early morning is your friend. If you can, set your alarm early and use the quiet time before the house stirs to get some work done.

4. **Signs for silence.** If you need to make calls that require business-like silence, tie a scarf to the door handle and tell your children that they can't come into the room when the scarf is on the door. If this is doomed to failure, you can always do what a client of mine does, and take calls in her car parked outside her house.

5. **Make time for fun.** If you feel you are not getting enough time with your loved ones, then schedule some time for fun. Create an adventure, visit a garden or park or go to the movies. Planning some activities in your diary will help you feel less torn between work and family. And it will reenergise you and refresh your perspective.

6. **Long amusements.** If you have young children at home when you're working, ensure they have an activity to keep them amused for a decent stretch of time. One activity that has worked particularly well for me over the years include creating a special movie afternoon, darkening the room, making popcorn and getting the kids to snuggle up – guaranteed peace and quiet for two hours.

Managing emergencies

Even with plans, priorities, and workbooks full of vision boards, life can get in the way and seemingly bring our progress to a halt. Illness of ourselves or loved ones, school holidays, and surprise visits can all erode our plans, time and energy.

If you are the one responsible for childcare, whether it be for the school run, school holidays or everyday after nursery, having three sources of childcare back-up will give you a strong safety net.

Try to anticipate what your arrangements are for the following scenarios:

- If you have a meeting in the school holidays, what is your plan to have the children looked after?
- If you run late from a meeting or get stuck in traffic, who else will pick up the children from school?
- If your nanny or babysitter is sick, who else could you call upon?

Do the research now on alternative childcare options. Try the resources listed below.

Childcare resources:
- www.Gumtree.com
- http://www.emergencychildcare.co.uk/
- https://www.myfamilycare.co.uk/

And it's not just the children

Life can throw at us very big curve balls. And when we run our own business, these can have a significant impact, more so than when we 'escape' to our job. I have said that your life becomes very entwined with your business, and when the curve balls come they can impact our confidence and motivation.

A few years ago my father died in unfortunate and unexpected circumstances. My grief was dark and prolonged. Leaving my family half a world away in New Zealand and returning to a cold, gloomy London in February didn't do anything to lift my spirits. And yes, the vision board I mentioned earlier in the book helped. But it wasn't enough to bypass my misery and start looking for new business and make sales calls. Result? The worst year ever for my business revenue.

Reflecting on that year, and my business, my big learning was that I needed to change my business model. I needed to stop selling my time for money and sell products instead. In that way, my business could scale and ultimately run without me.

Take some time now, as gloomy as it might seem, to think about what curve balls life could throw at you, and the subsequent impact on your business. Then consider what you could do or put in place to minimise their impact.

Doing this exercise may give you some insights into how you could run your business differently, that you may even decide to implement now.

Who has done it?

When you start your business, you will not be alone. There are many women who have created their own businesses and made it work with children.

Government sources estimate the number of women who own micro, small and medium businesses is 1.6 million in the UK[1]. Micro, small and medium businesses range from sole traders to companies with up to 50 employees.

There is a growing community of women entrepreneurs, at all stages of their start-up journey. Many of them started just like you – with an idea, a burning desire for a different life and the courage to make it happen.

---

1 (Source: ONS Statistics on Self-employed April–June 2008–2012, and Department on Business, Innovation and Skills, Small Business Survey 2012)

More often they are being featured in the media for their innovative ideas, their economic impact and of course, how they manage to do it. Whilst I advocate not comparing yourself to these women, I love reading their stories to discover what I can learn from their approach and to be inspired by their success. I know what it takes to invent an idea and then to take it to the world with scale.

Below are the stories of some true innovators taken from the press, most of whom you will be familiar with, I'm sure.

If you have a baby, you may even have one of these. Skibz Bibs are funky baby and toddler bibs. They are bandana shaped and look more like a junior fashion accessory than a dribble catch-all. Helen Bristol, founder of Skibz Bibs, was featured in an *MSN Money* article, recounting how she created the product and attained fantastic PR by celebrity babies wearing her creations.

Helen started the business in 2007 and now the bibs are sold globally, and in 500 UK retailers such as John Lewis and JoJo Maman Bebe. Employing 10 staff, she supports other working mothers by offering flexible and remote working.

Helen says she feels proud of what she's accomplished: '*I judge success by sales and reputation, so when I see Skibz in over 500 UK retailers, exported around the world, winning awards and being bought by celebrities, I do feel a small measure of success.*' (Taken from *MSN Money*, March 2012).

If you like to book events online, you have probably used Julia Hartz's business, Eventbrite. Created in 2006, co-founder and president Julia has created an online tool used by millions globally. She has two daughters aged one and five.

She discusses how life was with two young daughters and an exploding tech start-up. She balances it all by '*using the village approach to balancing the madness. My husband and I are extremely fortunate to have both of our moms within driving distance so they both play a big role in helping us with the day-to-day needs. We also prioritise our time with our daughters and that creates a nice balance to the other hours of the day when we are thinking about, talking about, or doing work. It takes courage to ask for and receive help – I'm glad I figured out how to do it by year 2 of my daughter's life!'* (Featured in '25 Women Start Ups to Watch', NYmomsworld.com, September 2011.)

The fashion blogger and creator of 'it' bags, the Cambridge Satchel Company was created by mother and daughter team, Freda Thomas and Julie Deane. Starting in 2008 from their kitchen table, they began with only £600. In early 2014, they secured £12.7 million investment to continue their success. Employing almost 100 people, the company turned over £13 million in 2013.

Julie Deane's inspiration for starting the bag company was her own children, who she wanted to send to private school but didn't have the funds at the time to do so. Featured in the FT's 'My First Million' series, she says: *'Having my boxer dog with me and spending time with my children are my biggest indulgences. I try to pick up the children from school every day and arrange my schedule to fit around my family.'* (Taken from 'My first million' interview series, FT.com, January 2014.)

A new device to help babies sleep better, Sweet Dreamers was invented by Lynda Harding, mother of six. The device simulates the comforting noises of the womb for the baby in its cot. She created Ewan the dream sheep, after struggling to get her own newborn to sleep. Her innovative product is sold in UK chains including John Lewis, Mothercare and Boots.

In an interview with *MSN Money*, she advises mothers who want to start a business to manage their time so that family don't come second: *'I think you do have to be really quite organised to switch between business and family demands. If you're in business mode all the time then you end up feeling really guilty.* (Taken from *MSN Money*, March 2012.)

As a mother, whether you work in a job or have your own business, there will always be conflicting demands on your time. I have learnt over the years that I can't be there always for the children, or my clients. And travelling abroad a lot for my business has meant I have missed significant events. Though I know other mums, in full-time employment, who also miss out.

There isn't a 'one size fits all' solution here. Determine what is best for you, and live by that.

Remember that you are also being an incredible role model for your children. A self-starter, full of ideas, initiative and energy! Not to mention business savviness, creativity and determination.

Personally, I think these are fabulous qualities for a child to see in action and learn from. They will forget that school play you missed but they will always have the memories of what you created.

Busy woman's shortcut

The famous author Shirley Conran wrote in her book *Superwoman*, 'Life is too short to stuff a mushroom.' Even though that book was published in the 1970s, that quote still resonates today.

Be clear on your priorities (you may want to revisit your values you defined in Chapter 1) and stick with them. It may be that you let your standards drop a little around the house, or your social calendar slows down for a while.

Practise saying 'no' to anything that doesn't fit with your priority list. It may take a while for this to feel comfortable but persevere, as you will need to seek out as much time as possible. This will then give you more time to spend on what is truly important to you.

And do hire a cleaner. Having that work taken off you means you will have that extra time to work on your business. And I know, that four hours of your time doing marketing, planning or business development, will reap you far more rewards than getting more familiar with the hoover and mop!

Be savvy

If you created your business to have more flexibility enabling you to spend more time with the children, then be true to that. Be proactive and create your schedule to allow for school drop-offs and pick-ups, plan ahead for school holidays or school concerts and events.

I know from my own experience how frustrating it is to sit in a meeting for my business, knowing that had my planning been better, I would be enjoying my daughter's school play. One of the huge pay-offs for having your own business is that you make the rules. Knowing that I could have been somewhere else in that moment did not sit well with me. It is an experience I hope you avoid.

Caution

It is human nature to compare ourselves with others. Stop this now.

We are inundated with messages daily about being better ... better mothers, better wives, fitter, slimmer, more successful, more fulfilled and the litany of improvements goes on and on.

Embrace your vision.

Accept and live your values completely.

Make a plan to attain your goals.

And do the work.

Comparing yourself to the ideals shown in the media is distracting. Subconsciously you start to think 'I am not enough'. This will slow you down and hamper your progress.

When you do view these ideals in the media, instead of comparing yourself, acknowledge them and their success, and ask yourself, 'What could I learn from them?' This is a much more positive approach and will keep you moving forward.

Final thoughts...

Starting a business is an amazing feat. You create something out of nothing; you contribute to yourself and your family and also to the economy as a whole. Your idea helps someone improve his or her situation. All in all you make a difference.

Give yourself the permission to be a success.

Believe that you have all you need to make the business fly, and that if you don't you will know how to find it.

Owning my business has been a massive personal development journey. I know I am not the woman I was when I started 10 years ago, and I know that this journey of personal change will continue.

Those shifts are also reflected in my business. It has changed its shape, location and value proposition as I have gained more clarity on what I want and how I can better serve my market.

I love working with clients to enable them to bring their idea to life. To create a business out of a mere thought. And to guide them through the journey of starting their new business.

Wherever you are in your start-up adventure, I wish you all the very best of success.

Here's to creating the life and business you enjoy, feel fulfilled by and allows you to prosper!

Warmly,
Wendy

I would love to hear about your journey!

You can connect with me:

Email: wendy@corporatecrossovers.com
Web: www.corporatecrossovers.com
Twitter: @wendy_kerr
Linked In: uk.linkedin.com/in/wendyrkerr/
Google +: +WendyKerr
Facebook Page: www.facebook.com/CorporateCrossovers
Facebook: www.facebook.com/wendyrkerr

What did you think of this book?

We're really keen to hear from you about this book, so that we can make our publishing even better.

Please log on to the following website and leave us your feedback.

It will only take a few minutes and your thoughts are invaluable to us.

www.pearsoned.co.uk/bookfeedback

Index